Bond
No.1 for exam success

D0530527

The Parents' Guide to the 11+

OXFORD
UNIVERSITY PRESS

OXFORD

UNIVERSITY PRESS

Great Clarendon Street, Oxford, OX2 6DP, United Kingdom

Oxford University Press is a department of the University of Oxford. It furthers the University's objective of excellence in research, scholarship, and education by publishing worldwide. Oxford is a registered trade mark of Oxford University Press in the UK and in certain other countries

British Library Cataloguing in Publication Data
Data available

978-0-1927-4230-8

10 9 8 7 6 5 4

Paper used in the production of this book is a natural, recyclable product made from wood grown in sustainable forests. The manufacturing process conforms to the environmental regulations of the country of origin.

Printed in China

Acknowledgements

Page make-up: Oxford Designers & Illustrators Ltd
Illustrations: Oxford Designers & Illustrators Ltd
Cover illustration: Lo Cole

Although we have made every effort to trace and contact all copyright holders before publication this has not been possible in all cases. If notified, the publisher will rectify any errors or omissions at the earliest opportunity.

Links to third party websites are provided by Oxford in good faith and for information only. Oxford disclaims any responsibility for the materials contained in any third party website referenced in this work.

The Parents' Guide to the 11+

Contents

PLACEMENT TESTS *(Central pull-out section)*
- Verbal Reasoning
- English
- Maths
- Non-verbal Reasoning

Notes on the author

Michellejoy Hughes is a qualified and experienced teacher. She studied for her BA and PGCE in English at Liverpool and then her MA in English at Lancaster. She has spent many years working as a teacher in Liverpool, preparing pupils for SATs, GCSEs and A-level exams and she has worked as an examiner in English for both Edexcel and AQA examination boards.

Michellejoy now teaches privately and here she combines her experience and knowledge in an easy to read step-by-step manual for parents whose children will be sitting the 11+ examination. Her pupils represent some of the best private, selective and state schools across the country and from a wide variety of backgrounds. All four 11+ subjects are studied by some of her pupils, while others are sitting just one 11+ subject. Some parents have been through the system before, while others have no prior knowledge of the 11+. All parents want to know whether their child actually stands a realistic chance of passing the entrance exam.

In order to prepare for the 11+, Michellejoy has used the Bond series to devise a range of initial Placement Tests which are provided here as a detachable section to test your child. She has also created numerous teaching and motivational aids, which she shares in this book.

Having real solutions that are used in practice every week to great success is a key element of this book. Michellejoy shares solutions to common problems and using this manual will ensure your child receives the best preparation for the 11+.

This book has been updated to reflect the differences that 11+ examination boards have in their tests and to reflect the changes within the National Curriculum today. We hope it will provide everything that you need to find your way around the 11+ system.

> ❝ My child was doing well enough at school but we knew he wouldn't pass the 11+ without some help and guidance. We came to Michellejoy and our son followed the easy step-by-step methods and he really enjoyed the learning experience. He was well prepared for the 11+ exam and we were thrilled when we received the results and he passed. He is now settled happily into the grammar school and we would whole heartedly recommend the teaching methods used. ❞

Introduction
The Bond 11+ Action Plan

- What is the 11+?
- Is my child bright enough?
- Does my child need tutoring?
- Who decides if my child should take the 11+?

- How do I prepare for the 11+?
- Isn't it cheating to tutor towards the 11+?
- Isn't the school enough to get my child through their exams?

11+

- What about the 13+ exam?
- What about special needs?
- What about summer birthdays?
- What happens after the exam?

- Should I go to an appeal?
- How do we choose the right school?
- Where can I find the answer to my questions about the 11+?

You've heard whispers about the 11+ and some parents have had their children with private tutors for years. The practice books available overwhelm you. What is it all about and what can you do to best prepare your child?

This book will take you step-by-step through the whole 11+ examination process. The detachable Placement Tests and easy marking scheme provided in this manual will help you to assess your child and to build a picture of their ability.

The exam strategy plans will guide you through the exam preparation whether you have 12 months, 6 months or 3 months, with advice if you have more or less time before your child sits the 11+ exam. The process includes tips to manage stress and to maintain motivation and helps to make this important time exciting and enjoyable for everyone.

This manual takes into account regional differences and the types of 11+ tests your child will take. Whether it is an LEA or selective grammar/ private school 11+ exam or Common Entrance Exams, you can find out what is expected of your child and of you. The book also guides you through the post-examination process and will help to prepare your child for secondary school and to support them when they are there.

The Parents' Guide to the 11+ aims to provide the answers to your questions and will take the mystery and confusion out of the 11+. Following this manual will help to provide the best chance your child has at passing the 11+ exam and beyond.

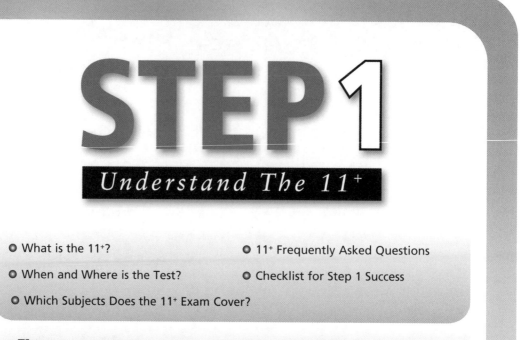

STEP 1
Understand The 11+

- What is the 11+?
- When and Where is the Test?
- Which Subjects Does the 11+ Exam Cover?
- 11+ Frequently Asked Questions
- Checklist for Step 1 Success

❝ I've overheard some of the parents talking about the 11+ and I know it's a test, but other than that, I'm not really sure what it's all about. The whole secondary school process seems confusing and I don't know who to talk to about it. I'm not even sure what questions to ask! ❞

❝ I've spent whole evenings on the Internet researching the 11+ and still can't find what I'm looking for. You go into a bookshop and there are loads of workbooks for children but nothing for parents. ❞

What is the 11⁺?

The 11⁺ is a selective entry examination for secondary school that children sit, usually during their school Year 6 or the summer term of Year 5. Due to changes in the law, the New School Admissions Code, schools now have to attempt to get results out before parents apply for a school. It does now mean that the 11⁺ test has to be brought forward, but this ruling does make it easier for parents when choosing a school. The other side to this is now more parents may consider entering their children for the 11⁺ exam as they have nothing to lose. This could potentially make the competition for places greater as it stops those situations where a parent does not enter their child for the 11⁺ because they are possibly borderline.

For some LEAs, the 11⁺ is taken during the school day in their primary school. In other parts of the country, the 11⁺ is organised by the selective and private schools and the exam is taken after school, or on a weekend, and takes place at the senior school. The 11⁺ is a means of testing children from an academic perspective and has no bearing on their SATs or GCSEs. Until the early 1970s all children took the 11⁺. It is no longer a compulsory test, but it continues to be used by the grammar and selective schools.

The 11⁺ exam differs throughout the country in terms of the subjects taken and also the examining board used. There are four subjects that can be tested in the 11⁺ exam. The subjects are verbal reasoning, non-verbal reasoning, English and maths. Sometimes these subjects are clearly divided into specific subjects and sometimes the exam is a combination of these subjects on the same paper. Although the maths and English tests tend to follow the National Curriculum, the verbal and non-verbal reasoning tests are not school-based subjects. Further information about the subjects tested can be found later in this section.

All of these tests can be either standard format (SF), which means that the answers are written out in full, or multiple-choice (MC) format, which offers a selection of answers for a child to choose from. This can be on the same exam paper, or on a separate answer paper. Some exams might include a mixture of standard and multiple choice formats. In some schools, one or more of the exams can take the form of a computer test, although this is more usually a reasoning paper that is sat before written exams. Although most 11⁺ tests are for Year 7 entrance at secondary school, in some of the private schools, the 11⁺ takes the form of a 'pre-13⁺' exam that must be passed, for pupils who begin their secondary school in Year 9.

Not all subjects are covered in every region so here is a guide to the LEAs and the subjects they test at 11⁺, with the time of year that they offer the 11⁺ exam. Some LEAs are listed more than once, which corresponds to grammar schools that have a different exam. For specific school information and for your LEA's contact details, see Appendix D found at www.bond11plus.co.uk in the Free Resources section. The following overview of LEAs and 11⁺ details was believed to be correct at the time of writing, but is always subject to change.

LEA	ENGLISH		MATHS		VR		NVR		Exam month	Exam type
	SF	MC	SF	MC	SF	MC	SF	MC		
Barnet Queen Elizabeth's		✓		✓					Sep	GL
Barnet St Michael's	✓	✓	✓	✓	✓	✓	✓	✓	Sep/Jan	CEM / Own
Bexley		✓		✓		✓		✓	Sep	CEM
Birmingham		✓		✓		✓		✓	Sep	CEM
Bournemouth	✓	✓		✓					Sep	GL
Bournemouth Girls'	✓	✓		✓		✓			Sep	GL
Bromley Newstead						✓		✓	Sep	GL
Bromley St Olave's		✓	✓						Sep	Own
Buckinghamshire		✓				✓		✓	Sep	CEM
Calderdale	✓			✓		✓			Oct	GL
Cumbria		✓				✓		✓	Sep	GL
Devon	✓			✓		✓			Oct	GL
Enfield Latymer		✓		✓		✓		✓	Sep	CEM
Essex Chelmsford Girls'		✓		✓		✓		✓	Sep	CEM
Essex Consortium Schools	✓		✓		✓		✓		Sep	Own
Essex King John						✓			Sep	GL
Gloucestershire		✓		✓		✓		✓	Sep	CEM
Hertfordshire Consortium			✓		✓			✓	Sep	GL / Moray
Kent		✓		✓		✓		✓	Sep	GL
Kingston-upon-Thames Tiffin						✓			Oct	GL
Kingston-upon-Thames Tiffin Girls'	✓		✓			✓		✓	Oct/Nov	GL / Own
Kirklees		✓		✓		✓		✓	Sep	CEM
Lancashire		✓		✓		✓			Sep	GL / Own
Lincolnshire Caistor					✓	✓			Sep	GL
Lincolnshire Consortium					✓		✓		Sep	GL
Liverpool		✓		✓				✓	Oct	GL / Own
Medway	✓			✓		✓			Sep	GL
Northern Ireland AQE	✓		✓						Nov	CEA
Northern Ireland PPT		✓		✓					Nov	GL
North Yorkshire Ermysted & Ripon							✓	✓	Sep	GL

LEA	ENGLISH		MATHS		VR		NVR		Exam month	Exam type
	SF	MC	SF	MC	SF	MC	SF	MC		
North Yorkshire Skipton		✓		✓		✓			Oct	GL
Plymouth		✓		✓					Sep	GL / Own
Poole		✓		✓		✓		✓	Oct	GL
Poole Parkstone		✓		✓		✓			Oct	GL
Reading Boys'		✓		✓		✓		✓	Sep	CEM
Reading Girls'	✓				✓		✓		Oct	GL
Reading Kendrick	✓		✓		✓		✓		Sep	CEM
Redbridge		✓		✓		✓		✓	Sep	CEM
Shropshire Consortium	✓	✓	✓	✓	✓	✓	✓	✓	July	CEM
Slough	✓	✓	✓	✓	✓	✓	✓	✓	Sep	CEM
Southend on Sea	✓		✓		✓		✓		Sep	Own
Sutton Grammar Group	✓	✓	✓	✓					Sep/Nov	Own
Sutton Nonsuch Girls'	✓		✓						Sep/Oct	Own
Trafford Altrincham Boys'		✓		✓		✓			Sep	GL
Trafford Altrincham Girls'		✓		✓		✓			Sep	GL
Trafford Loreto	✓	✓	✓			✓			Sep	GL
Trafford Sale				✓		✓		✓	Sep	CEM
Trafford St Ambrose		✓		✓		✓			Sep	GL
Trafford Stretford	✓			✓		✓		✓	Sep	GL
Trafford Urmston		✓		✓				✓	Sep	GL
Walsall	✓	✓	✓	✓	✓	✓	✓	✓	July	CEM
Warwickshire	✓	✓	✓	✓	✓	✓	✓	✓	Sep	CEM
Wiltshire		✓		✓		✓			Sep	GL
Wirral						✓			Sep	GL
Wirral St Anselm's Boys'	✓		✓	✓					Sep	Own
Wirral Upton Girls'						✓			Sep	GL
Wolverhampton Consortium	✓	✓	✓	✓	✓	✓	✓	✓	July	CEM

✓ HINT

It is vital that you confirm with your choice of school:

- *when the 11+ is,*
- *which subjects are tested,*
- *what format the exams take,*
- *who provides the exam.*

LEAs or schools can, and do, change their 11+ exams and finding the answer to these questions is your first step on your 11+ journey.

Private Schools

Private schools may use the Common Entrance Exam (CEE) or their own exams as an alternative to the standard 11⁺ exams. The CEE is set by the Independent Schools Examinations Board (ISEB) and the papers set will be exactly the same for all schools who use it. At 11⁺ it can consist of papers in English, maths and science as the core subjects, but other subjects, especially at the 13⁺ level, can be included such as history, geography, religion, Latin and Greek. Some schools have formed consortiums so that a child can sit one exam in one school but can then apply for any of the schools within the consortium. If a private school is using the CEE, it is most commonly taken in January, but this isn't always the case so do contact the schools in plenty of time to check whether they use the CEE or set their own and to confirm the time of year. This information is usually in their current school prospectus. It is usually possible to get past papers from the school to use as revision. See Appendix D (found at www.bond11plus.co.uk) for further details.

Which Subjects Does the 11⁺ Exam Cover?

Verbal Reasoning

Verbal reasoning tests are popular as they are a good indication of potential academic ability. They test children's problem solving skills while working quickly and accurately, and how effectively they can process information. Verbal reasoning tests a child's knowledge of vocabulary and spellings. Verbal reasoning tests can be broken into four main sections: Selecting Words, Sorting Words, Codes and Sequences, Verbal and Numerical Logic.

Let's have a look at these main sections and the question types that are covered:

Selecting Words
- Identify groups of words
- Sort words into categories
- Pair up words
- Make compound words
- Find words that do not belong
- Find words that are most similar
- Find words that are most opposite
- Find words that have letters in common
- Add a prefix or suffix for a set of words
- Add or take a letter to make new words
- Add letters to complete a word

Sorting Words
- Rearrange letters to make a word
- Rearrange a sentence to make sense of it
- Rearrange a sentence to find the superfluous word
- Complete crosswords
- Put words in alphabetical order
- Find a word hidden in a sentence
- Find a small word in a larger word
- Anagrams

Verbal Reasoning Question Types

Codes and Sequences
- Work out letter and number sequences
- Code and decode words using letters
- Code and decode words using numbers
- Code and decode words using symbols
- Use number triplets
- Use letter triplets

Verbal and Numerical Logic
- Make deductions from given information
- Apply number logic
- Use a rule to create new words
- Number substitution
- Balance equations

Selecting Words

These questions are all about word recognition and definition. Can your child identify words that are similar or different? Out of a given group of words can your child work out which is the odd one out? Some questions require a child to organise words into categories or to find a common link between words. Below are some examples of selecting words questions.

 HINT

Common problems stem from a lack of word knowledge. Reading, word games and dictionary games will help your child to answer these types of questions.

1 In these questions, your child is asked to select the best-fit answer.

> Big is to small as tall is to (narrow, short, high).
> Jumper is to wool as shirt is to (cotton, white, smooth).
> Cat is to kitten as horse is to (calf, foal, animal).
>
> *Answers: short, cotton, foal*

The **skill** required here is for your child to have an understanding of the relationship between words, to be able to put words into pairs and to recognise opposites, similarities or how words are connected in some way. The **strategy** needed is for your child to keep asking, 'What is the link between the first pair?' When they can find the answer (big is opposite to small), they need to keep the same pattern in the second set of words: 'Tall is opposite to short'.

> **TRY THIS!**
>
> Play word games with your child where you suggest a word and tell them to find a word that is opposite and then similar to it, or a game where you suggest a pair of words and your child tries to find the common link. This can really help with the second example here where a child might know that jumper and wool are not opposite or similar but if they can find another link, i.e. Jumpers can be made out of wool, the following pairing is made easier.

2 Select two words, one from each bracket, that are most similar.

> (liquid, soft, fixed)   (rough, fluid, melt)
> (sing, melody, music)   (laugh, instrument, tune)
> (dear, customer, buy)   (expensive, gift, present)
>
> *Answers: liquid/fluid, melody/tune, dear/expensive*

 HINT

Thinking in a logical manner is the technique your child needs to learn in order to be able to perform well at the 11⁺. These thought patterns, which might seem long-winded at first, will soon become second nature.

The **skill** required here is knowledge of vocabulary and synonyms; to know the definition of words and which ones are most similar in meaning. The **strategy** here is to pair the first word of the first bracket with the words in the second bracket and then the second word of the first bracket with words in the second bracket, etc. For example:

Liquid is rough, soft is rough, fixed is rough
Well none of these make sense and so rough can be rejected.

Liquid is melt, soft is melt, fixed is melt
Well none of these make sense and so melt can be rejected.

Liquid is fluid, soft is fluid, fixed is fluid
*Now we have our answer: **Liquid is fluid**.*

(3) Select two words that are the odd ones out.

> **Q** blue, sky, white, clouds, green
> toffee, coffee, sweets, milk, tea
> football, kit, player, cricket, rounders
>
> *Answers: sky and clouds, toffee and sweets, kit and player*

The **skills** required here are to find the common link between words and the ability to recognise the most appropriate link between groups of words. The **strategy** can be difficult for the more creative child, as it can be easy to find links. For example, in the first question a child might choose 'green' and 'clouds' as the odd words out because the sky is blue and white, or they might select 'green' and 'white' because the sky is blue and has clouds. It is therefore important for the child to consider which link provides a definite group, e.g. blue, white and green are all colours; therefore sky and clouds are the odd ones out. It isn't just about finding any linking word; it is about finding *the strongest link* between **the group of words**.

Sorting Words

This section is about recognising how a word can be constructed. Does your child understand how sentences are constructed? Can they find words hidden between other words using the beginning letters and end letters of other words? Can they solve anagrams or place words in alphabetical order? Below are some typical sorting words questions.

(1) Place these words into the longest sentence possible to find the superfluous word.

> **Q** Carrots cabbage of lots rabbit pet orange her she gave.
> It's to give books the library local from borrow handy.
> Football the balloon up the air into floated red.
>
> *Answers: Cabbage (she gave her pet rabbit lots of orange carrots)*
> *Give (it's handy to borrow books from the local library), football (the red balloon floated up into the air)*

The **skills** required here are finding the gist of the sentence and rearranging the words to recognise which word is superfluous. A useful **strategy** is to read out the words, then to look away and to consider what the words are trying to say. Which words go together and which word seems odd? For example, in the first sentence 'orange carrots' and 'pet rabbit' go together and by building these little units, it reduces our options and so make the sentence much easier to see. Placing 'carrots' next to 'cabbage' is trying to lead us towards vegetables, but as soon as we read about pet rabbits, we realise it is not about vegetables and the word 'orange' gives us another clue. Therefore, reading through the sentence first can help us not to fall into these types of word traps!

2 Find a four letter word hidden between two consecutive words.

> **Q** It is a bit late to visit the farm anyway.
> The family were excited as they walked to the Mosque.
> I need to use the iron to press this suit.
>
> *Answers: many (farm anyway), them (the Mosque), heir (the iron)*

The **skill** required here is to see the letters of each word as separate elements that can be used to create a four letter word. A useful **strategy** is to remember that we can either use three letters at the end of the first word plus one letter at the beginning of the second word OR two letters at the end of the first word plus two letters at the beginning of the second word OR one letter at the end of the first word plus three letters at the beginning of the second word. Using our pencil or fingers, we can block off the letters that we don't need and focus our attention on the letters that we do need like this:

I **tol**d him that not everyone is here? itol isn't a word
I **told h**im that not everyone is here? oldh isn't a word
I to**ld hi**m that not everyone is here? ldhi isn't a word
I tol**d him** that not everyone is here? dhim isn't a word
I told **him th**at not everyone is here? imth isn't a word
I told hi**m tha**t not everyone is here? mtha isn't a word
I told him **that n**ot everyone is here? hatn isn't a word
I told him th**at no**t everyone is here? atno isn't a word
I told him tha**t not** everyone is here? tnot isn't a word
I told him that **not e**veryone is here? Note is a word – we've found our answer!

3 Place the following words in reverse alphabetical order.

> **Q** Porous, pores, poorly, poor, portly
>
> *Answers: Portly, porous, pores, poorly, poor*

> **✓ HINT**
>
> *Remember to read the question properly as it might have 'alphabetical order' or 'reverse alphabetical order'.*

The **skill** required here is to place the words in the opposite order to that found in a dictionary. A useful **strategy** is to place the words under each other so that it is easier to compare the letters. We can then see which words would come last in the dictionary, like this:

p	o	r	o	u	s
p	o	r	e	s	
p	o	o	r	l	y
p	o	o	r		
p	o	r	t	l	y

Space the words out to make it easier to read the letters up and down.

p	o	r	o	u	s
p	o	r	e	s	
p	o	o	r	l	y
p	o	o	r		
p	o	r	t	l	y

We can cross out the first two columns as they are the same, then we can see 'r' is after 'o' in the third column.

p	o	r	o	u	s
p	o	r	e	s	
p	o	o	r	l	y
p	o	o	r		
p	o	r	t	l	y

Looking in the fourth column we can now order the first three words: portly, porous and pores.

p	o	r	o	u	s
p	o	r	e	s	
p	o	o	r	l	y
p	o	o	r		
p	o	r	t	l	y

Going back to the remaining two words, we can see in the fourth column that 'poor' is now a complete word so it would come before poorly in the dictionary. We're looking in reverse order so we now have our final two words: poorly then poor.

Does your child know the alphabet? There is a huge difference between recognising the alphabet and knowing it. Try some quick fire questions such as 'What's 8 letters before 'T'? 'What's 3 letters after 'J'? Try learning the alphabet backwards as well as forwards so that letter work becomes quicker and easier. Encourage your child to create some anagrams – it doesn't matter if they want to do anagrams on birds, colours, girls' names or boy bands, it is playing with letters that is the skill.

Codes and Sequences

This section is about recognising how letters and numbers can be coded, decoded and sequenced. Does your child know their alphabet? Do they know their multiplication tables? Can they recognise prime numbers, square numbers, cube numbers, Fibonacci sequences? Below are some typical code and sequence questions.

(1) Complete each sequence. The alphabet is here to help you.

A B C D E F G H I J K L M N O P Q R S T U V W X Y Z

AC	DF	GI	JL	_____	_____
144	_____	100	_____	64	49
AZ	CX	_____	GT	_____	KP

Answers: MO, PR   121, 81   EV, IR

The **skill** required for this question type is to find the logic pattern between the letters or numbers, and then to complete the same pattern to solve the question. The **strategy** for the letter sequences is to look at the links between the first letter of each set and then the next. It's important not to get confused by looking at the sequence of the letters together, but in relation to the other groups of letters. In the first example, this means **not** to look at the relationship between A and C or D and F but to look at the relationship between A and D and then C and F like this:

A to D = (+3) D to G = (+3) G to J = (+3)   We now know that our first letter must be J (+3) = M

C to F = (+3) F to I = (+3) I to L = (+3)   We now know that our second letter must be L (+3) = O

The **strategy** for the number sequences is to recognise the relationship between the numbers and to copy that same pattern. Knowing primes, square and cube numbers and the Fibonacci sequence numbers is useful for solving this question type.

TRY THIS!

These patterns are best learnt 'parrot fashion' so that these questions become much easier:

Primes   (a number divisible only by '1' and the number itself)
           1, 2, 3, 5, 7, 11, 13, 17, 19, 23, 29, 31

Squares   (a number multiplied by itself)
           1, 4, 9, 16, 25, 36, 49, 64, 81, 100, 121, 144

Cubes   (a number multiplied by itself then by itself again)
           1, 8, 27, 64, 125, 216, 343, 512, 729, 1000

Fibonacci (1st number + 2nd number = 3rd number) 1, 1, 2, 3, 5, 8, 13, 21,
           34, 55, 89, 144

(2) Solve the following code and decode questions. The alphabet is given to help you.

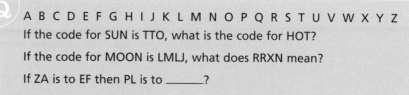

A B C D E F G H I J K L M N O P Q R S T U V W X Y Z

If the code for SUN is TTO, what is the code for HOT?

If the code for MOON is LMLJ, what does RRXN mean?

If ZA is to EF then PL is to _____?

Answers: INU, STAR, UQ

 HINT

These codes might have a regular pattern such as +1 −1 or +1, +2, +3 etc. but sometimes the relationship is more random like the 3rd example. As long as the technique is followed, the answer is easy enough to find.

The **skill** required for this question type is to recognise the relationship between letters and to complete this pattern to solve the question. Sometimes it is to find a code, and sometimes it is to decode a word. The **strategy** is similar to the sequences in that it is important to work from the first letter of the first word and to the first letter of the second word and not between letters of each word. Here is an example:

As we have two words and one code, we work from the word to the code like this:

S − T = +1 so H +1 = I
U − T = −1 so O −1 = N
N − O = +1 so T +1 = U
If SUN = TTO then HOT = INU

(3) The middle word has been formed by the two words each side of it. Follow the same pattern to find the middle word in the second set:

master (male) learn   rested (_____) apple

bugle (ugly) fairly   girl (_____) upon

play (sway) swim   look (_____) bore

Answers: reap, iron, book

The **skill** required here is an ability to follow patterns and to recognise the order of letters within a word. The **strategy** for answering this type of question is to try numbering each letter in the two outside words to find which number sequence is used and then copy this pattern with the second group of words like this:

1st	**M**		1st	**R**	
2nd	**A**		2nd	**E**	
3rd	**S**		3rd	**S**	
4th	**T**	**M** = 1st	4th	**T**	1st = **R**
5th	**E**	**A** = 2nd or 9th	5th	**E**	2nd and 9th = **E** or P
6th	**R**	**L** = 7th	6th	**D**	7th = **A**
7th	**L**	**E** = 5th or 8th	7th	**A**	5th and 8th = E or **P**
8th	**E**		8th	**P**	
9th	**A**		9th	**P**	
10th	**R**		10th	**L**	
11th	**N**		11th	**E**	

We can now see the combination of letters that will make a word. **REAP**

(**4**) The middle number has been formed by the two outside numbers. Find the pattern that has been used in the first and second triplet and repeat this pattern to solve the final triplet.

30 (40) 50	25 (30) 35	16 (_____) 60
5 (11) 6	9 (40) 11	4 (_____) 8
100 (73) 3	80 (16) 4	90 (_____) 2

Answers: 38 ((16 + 60) ÷ 2), 48 ($8^2 - 4^2$), 82 ($90 - 2^3$)

The **skill** here is to recognise how the middle number has been created and to use the same pattern to solve the final triplet. The **strategy** is to look at the first triplet and to see how the middle number can be made using either one step (multiplication, division, addition, subtraction of the numbers given, the square, the cube or the root of the numbers), or more than one step (most commonly to then halve, double, add/subtract/multiply/divide by 2, 5 or 10).

Once a pattern has been found, the same pattern can be used with the second triplet and if this gives the same answer, the final triplet can be solved.

||||➡ TRY THIS!

This question type often looks tricky, but working logically with the first triplet is crucial. One technique that I use with my pupils is to get them to form an equation like this:

30 (40) 50   30 + 50 = 80   50 – 30 = 20   50 × 30 = 1500

Now I can see that 80 is double 40 and 20 is half of 40 so here are two possible equations:

(30 + 50) ÷ 2 = 40   (50 – 30) × 2 = 40

Next step is to try these same two equations using the numbers from the second triplet:

(25 + 35) ÷ 2 = 30   (35 – 25) × 2 = 20

It is now easy to see that the first equation works so we can solve the third triplet:

(16 + 60) ÷ 2 = **38**

This section is about logical thinking to find an answer. Can your child follow complex instructions? Can they use a rule to create a word? How are they at number substitution or deducing critical information from a series of statements? Here are some typical verbal and numerical logic question types.

① Solve the following equations.

> **Q** If A = 1, B = 2, C = 4, D = 8 and E = 12 write these answers as letters.
>
> C + D = E ÷ ?
>
> 2C × 5B = 6E + ?
>
> BCD ÷ C² = ?
>
> *Answers: A (4 + 8 = 12 ÷ 1 = A) D (8 × 10 = 72 + 8 = D)*
> *C ((2 × 4 × 8) ÷ 16 = 4 = C)*

The **skills** required for this question are an ability to interchange letters and numbers and to understand how substitution works. The **strategy** for this question is to rewrite the equation exchanging numbers for the letters, work out the sum and then convert the numbers back to letters.

② Read the following information and then answer the question.

> **Q** Jenny, Jodie, Jon, Jamil and Jordan are 10, 9, 8, 7 and 6 years old, but not in this order.
> Jamil is 1 year younger than Jon. Jordan is older than Jenny. Jodie is 2 years younger than Jon.
> Jenny is 2 years younger than Jodie. Who is the youngest?
>
> *Answer: Jenny is the youngest.*

The **skill** required here is being able to recognise facts that bear relation to other clues and the ability to deduct maximum information from each clue. The **strategy** is to create a logical system for working out each relation. Take each sentence and, in turn, work out all the information that can be gained from it. A simple grid can be used here like this:

	10	9	8	7	6
Jenny	X				
Jodie					
Jon					X
Jamil	X				
Jordan					X

Jamil is 1 year younger than Jon so Jamil cannot be 10 and John cannot be 6.

Jordan is older than Jenny so Jordan cannot be 6 and Jenny cannot be 10.

	10	9	8	7	6
Jenny	X	X	X	X	✓
Jodie	X	X	✓	X	X
Jon				X	X
Jamil	X				
Jordan					X

Jodie is 2 years younger than Jon so Jodie can't be 9 or 10 and Jon can't be 6 or 7.

Jenny is 2 years younger than Jodie, so Jodie cannot be 6 or 7 and Jenny cannot be 9 or 10 so Jodie must be 8 and this means that Jenny must be 6 so she is the youngest.

It is easy to consider other pieces of information. For example in the previous question, you could work out how old everyone is, but the question only requires you to know who the youngest is.

(3) **Read the following information and then find the statement that must be true.**

> **Q** Mr Rajinder's wife's mother is called Rani and it is her birthday next Tuesday.
>
> a) Mr Rajinder's wife is called Rani.
> b) Mr Rajinder's mother is called Rani Rajinder.
> c) Mr Rajinder's mother-in-law has a birthday next Tuesday.
> d) Rani was born on a Tuesday.
>
> *Answer: c – Mr Rajinder's mother-in-law has a birthday next Tuesday.*

The **skill** in this question type is to understand the meaning of each fact and to unravel the information to find the true statement. The **strategy** is to work backwards and check each statement against the information given like this:

Is Mr Rajinder's wife called Rani? *No – his wife's mother is called Rani, we don't know his wife's name.*

Is Mr Rajinder's mother-in-law called Rani Rajinder? *No – her first name is Rani but we don't know her surname.*

Does Mr Rajinder's mother-in-law have a birthday next Tuesday? *Yes! Mr Rajinder's wife's mother is his mother-in-law and she does have a birthday next Tuesday.*

All of these question types are explained in further detail in *Bond How To Do 11+ Verbal Reasoning*, which can be bought or ordered from most bookshops. (See Appendix B for details.)

Non-verbal Reasoning

Non-verbal reasoning tests look at patterns and shape rather than words and verbal processes. They test children's problem solving skills while working quickly and accurately, and how effectively they can process information through graphic or pictorial representation. Non-verbal reasoning tests can be broken into four sections: Identifying Shapes, Missing Shapes, Rotating Shapes and Coded Shapes.

Let's have a look in more detail at each section and understand how you can help your child succeed at non-verbal reasoning.

Identifying Shapes
- Identify shapes
- Identify patterns
- Pair up shapes
- Recognise shapes that are similar

Missing Shapes
- Find a given part within a shape
- Find a missing shape from a pattern
- Find shapes that complete a sequence

Non-verbal Reasoning Question Types

Rotating Shapes
- Recognise mirror images
- Relate shapes to given nets
- Link nets to cubes

Loaded Shapes
- Code and decode shapes using letters
- Code and decode shapes using numbers
- Apply shape logic

Identifying shapes

This section develops the visual recognition of shape and pattern. Can your child recognise symbols and shapes that are alike? Can they sort shapes by colour, direction, size and number of sides? Typical identifying shapes questions might include the following examples.

(1) **The first two shapes are related in some way. Can you circle the fourth shape that is related to the third in the same way as the second is related to the first?**

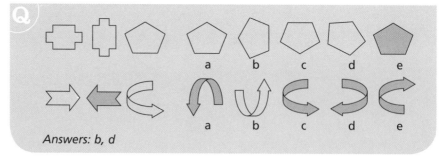

Answers: b, d

The **skill** required for this type of question is an understanding of what has changed between the first two shapes. Once this connection is made, the same connection can be applied to the next set of shapes. The **strategy** is to create a logical pattern of questioning, for example in the second question.

The second shape has changed colour and is pointing in the opposite direction from the first shape.

Now we are looking for a changed colour and opposite direction version of this third shape.

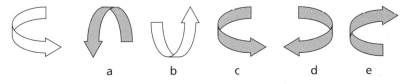

a   b   c   d   e

Shape a has changed colour, but is not an opposite direction.
Shape b hasn't changed colour and isn't an opposite direction.
Shape c has changed colour, but hasn't changed direction.
Shape d has changed colour and it is in an opposite direction.
Shape e has changed colour, but is not an opposite direction.

We can now see that shape d is the answer.

▐▐▐▶ TRY THIS!

A technique that I use with my pupils is the **SPANOS** checklist to see how a shape can be altered.

Size (smaller, larger?)
Position (transposed higher, lower, the same?)
Angle (rotated, reflected?)
Number (number of sides, corners, bars, dots?)
Outline (new shape, flattened shape, extended shape?)
Shading (colour, pattern?)

② **Circle the two shapes that are identical.**

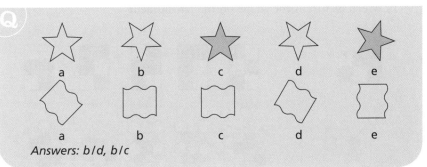

a   b   c   d   e

a   b   c   d   e

Answers: b/d, b/c

The **skill** required in this question is the ability to match alike shapes by recognising what selected shapes have in common. The **strategy** is to take note of the direction, size and colour of the shapes and to exclude any shape that is obviously unrelated. This should help to identify the exact match.

(3) Circle the one odd shape out.

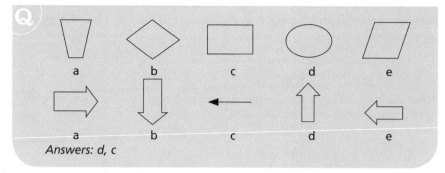

Answers: d, c

The **skill** tested here is the ability to work out a relationship that links four of the shapes together leaving an odd one out. The **strategy** required is to first try looking at common areas such as colour, type of shape (all straight edges, has four sides, are based on a circle, etc.), size and direction.

For example, in the first question all shapes have four edges except for the oval; in the second question all shapes are block arrows except for c.

> **TRY THIS!**
>
> Any games that help with pattern and shape are fantastic training for these question types. Tile shape patterns, jigsaw puzzles (real or 'online'), even
>
> 'spot the difference' games are great for honing these skills and adding variety to assessment papers.

Missing shapes

This section develops spatial awareness and understanding of rotation. Can your child recognise patterns within a pattern? Can they recognise a pattern when it is rotated, reflected, transposed? Typical missing shapes questions include the following examples.

(1) In which picture is the shape on the left hidden?

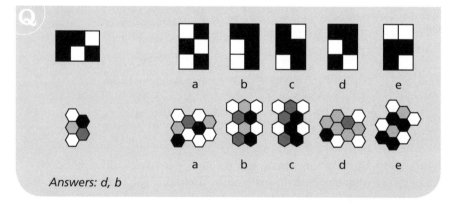

Answers: d, b

The **skills** required here are the ability to recognise shapes (identifying individual parts of a larger shape and being able to find exact matches) and the ability to rotate shapes mentally. The **strategy** needed is to work from left to right looking for identical elements and this can be easier if the partial shape is broken down further. In question 1 for example:

- Look for two diagonal black squares.
- Check if the two diagonal black squares have two white diagonal squares opposite to them.

This systematic approach is more effective and quicker than staring at each shape hoping the answer will appear, especially when the shapes might be in a rotated form.

TRY THIS!

It might be easier to rotate the sheet of paper so that you can see the pattern in its rotated form. If it helps, try to find a way of describing the pattern to fix it into your memory. Some of my more creative pupils have seen 'an ice cream with a drip' and 'a dog with an elephant's trunk' as description that has helped them to find the right answer. In question 1, my favourite description was 'a man praying'!

Rotating Shapes

This section looks at the nets of cubes and how objects look when they are rotated. Here is an example of a typical rotating shape question:

(1) **Which one of the nets on the right is the only one that can be made into the cube on the left?**

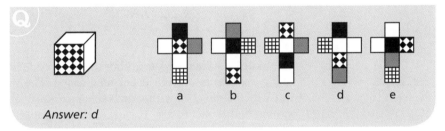

a   b   c   d   e

Answer: d

The **skill** here is to work out how the cube will look as a net by considering colour, pattern and the position of each face in relation to each other. The **strategy** is to visualise each net rebuilt as a cube. Which colour face goes where? By working out how each face fits systematically, the answer becomes easier to find. There are some critical rules that can help with nets and cubes:

Opposite faces can never be seen together so the two white faces on the cube must be together. This means that net 'c' is rejected and because there is only one white face on net 'b', we have to reject this net.

Faces that join together in a cube have to be joined together in the net. This means that on net 'e' the diamond shape must be joined to the white face but here they are opposites so we can reject net 'e'.

Make sure that directions of arrows, stripes and blocks are facing in the same direction.

Make sure that the background and the foreground are the same. For example, the diamond shape on the cube is black diamond on a white background, but in net 'a' it is a white diamond on a black background so we have to reject this net.

> ✓ **HINT**
>
> *Cubes and nets are notoriously difficult so have a go at making your own cubes. Take a piece of paper and create the six faces of the net. Now decorate each face with a different pattern and then fold the net up into a cube securing each face with some sticky tape. Now have a look at which faces are seen together and which are not as you rotate the cube. The more you can do this, the easier it is to picture the net and cube.*

Coded Shapes

This section considers the connection between shapes and letters or shapes and numbers using codes to find relationships. Typical coded shapes questions include the following.

(1) **Complete the code for the last shape.**

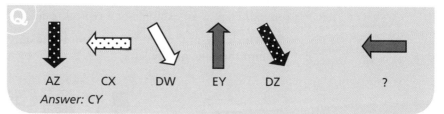

| AZ | CX | DW | EY | DZ | ? |

Answer: CY

The **skills** required are the ability to pair a code with a shape and the ability to then interpret the encoded shape. The **strategy** here is to work out which code goes with which shape, colour, size or direction. A logical system makes this easier. For example, we could follow a thought-process like this:

1ˢᵗ arrow = South	and **Black Dotty**	A and Z	
2ⁿᵈ arrow = West	and White Dotty	C and X	
3ʳᵈ arrow = **South East**	and White	D and W	
4ᵗʰ arrow = North	and Grey	E and Y	
5ᵗʰ arrow = **South East**	and **Black Dotty**	D and Z	

We can see that **Z** must stand for **black dotty**, so we know the second letter represents the pattern. We can see that **D** must stand for **south east** so the first letter represents the arrow's direction.

All of these question types are explained in further detail in *Bond How To Do 11⁺ Non-verbal Reasoning*, which can be bought or ordered from most bookshops. (See Appendix B for details.)

English

The 11⁺ English tests cover the elements of reading and writing. They examine how effectively a child can understand and use the English language. But what does this really mean? English tests can be broken into five sections: Comprehension, Spellings, Punctuation and Grammar, Vocabulary, and Word Choice. Let's have a look at these areas in more detail.

Spellings:
- Fill in missing letters
- Put words into alphabetical order
- Recognise misspelt words
- Tricky words

Comprehension:
- Read for understanding
- Take answers from a text
- Understand beyond the text
- Recognise proverbs and sayings
- Match words and definitions

Punctuation and Grammar:
- Word classes
- Punctuation
- Tenses
- Using conjunctions

English Question Types

Vocabulary:
- Homophones and homonyms
- Singular and plurals
- Antonyms and synonyms

Word Choice:
- Context
- Cloze tests
- Anagrams
- Mixed-up letters
- Word fit

Let's have a look in more detail at each section and understand how you can help your child succeed at English.

Comprehension

This section is all about reading and understanding information that is given in a text. Is your child a strong reader? Do they pick up written information quickly and efficiently? Some questions require a child to understand common English proverbs and sayings. Here are some examples of comprehension questions based on this short extract from a fairy story.

Monster at My Window

Megan was not brave enough to peep from under the duvet. She knew the monster was waiting for her. Megan had called for help but when her brother Ryan had come in, he had teased her, 'There's nothing at the window you silly baby. Look!' He had pulled back the curtain and sure enough, there was nothing there. The wind was making the pear tree branches creak and groan and in a strong squall the tips of the twigs swished against the window frame like a horse whip, but other than that, the night was certainly not the centre stage for monsters and ghosts. Ryan pulled the curtains together and went back to his room laughing, but Megan didn't feel reassured. Eventually, she took a steady breath and appeared from under the bedcover. Clearly against her thin, pink curtains, she could see the silhouette of the monster's spiky, long arms moving about. She could see the sharp pins in the monster's arms and she could hear it moaning her name. It was going to get her. She could hear the monster knocking on the window, trying to get in. Megan screamed...

(1) **Which one of these statements is true?**

a) The branches were blown by the rain.
b) The twigs touched the window frame.
c) There were pears on the tree.
d) The leaves creaked and groaned.

Answer: b

The **skill** required is for your child to read the text and to understand what is happening. The **strategy** needed is for your child to read the text carefully in order to understand what is written and to look for the answers to the questions. It is important for a child to find keywords to find the sections of the extract needed.

(2) **Which word could have been used instead of 'silhouette'?**

a) Noise
b) Echo
c) Outline
d) Darkness

Answer: c

The **skill** required is for a child to understand the meaning of the word and to find another similar word. The **strategy** is for a child to be able to find a specific word in the extract, to read the word in context, which provides a range of clues, and to then consider another word that could be used that would have the same meaning.

(3) **What type of text is this taken from? Find four pieces of evidence to support your answer.**

_____

_____

_____

Answer: (1 mark) it is a fictional story. Any four of the following: (1 mark) It is written as free-flowing prose so it is isn't a poem or play script. (1 mark) It is written in the third person with characters so it isn't a factual piece. (1 mark) The extract is telling a story for entertainment. (1 mark) The extract uses literary effects such as onomatopoeia and similes.

Word definition is important for this. The *Bond Spelling and Vocabulary* books are useful for extending a child's vocabulary and a child's encyclopaedia can help to extend general knowledge. Quizzes, dictionary games and crosswords will all help to extend knowledge. (See Appendix B for further details.)

Spellings

This section is all about spellings and word choice. Does your child have a high spelling age? Do they easily remember spelling 'rules'? How do they perform at their school spelling tests? Here are some typical spelling related questions:

1 In these sentences there are either no spelling mistakes or one spelling mistake. Underline the sentences that do have spelling mistakes and write the correct spelling in the box on the right.

Q
a) Charlotte was not aware of the darkness that engulfed her. | a)
b) She could see only the bright light in the distance. | b)
c) Foecusing on the light she carefully got up. | c)
d) Holding onto the wall for suport, she moved slowly. | d)

Answer: c (Focusing) d (support)

The **skill** required in this question is an ability to recognise incorrect and correct spellings of words. Sometimes it will be an individual word that is given and sometimes a complete sentence so careful reading is needed. The **strategy** is to gain spelling knowledge and to recognise common errors in spelling. Reading can help develop this strategy as can remembering common spelling rules.

2 Add the missing letters in these words so that the word on the right has an opposite meaning to the word on the left.

Q
a) selfish   s _ _ _ _ _ _ s
b) ascended   d _ _ _ _ _ _ _ d
c) domesticated f _ _ _ l

Answers: a) selfless   b) descended   c) feral

The **skill** required in this question is an ability to work out the word most opposite and to then spell it correctly. The **strategy** is to think of any word that could be an opposite to the word on the left and to then match the word against the number of letters in the word, and with the letters already given.

(3) Underline the correctly spelt word in each sentence.

> **Q**
> a) We had a school trip to the (cathedral, cathederal, catherdral).
>
> b) Afterwards we had our lunch in the (restaraunt, resterant, restaurant).
>
> c) Finally we (traveled, travalled, travelled) back to school in the coach.
>
> *Answers: a) cathedral   b) restaurant   c) travelled*

The **skill** required in this question is an ability to recognise the correct spellings of words. The **strategy** is to gain spelling knowledge and to recognise common errors in spelling. Reading can again help to develop this strategy as can remembering common spelling rules.

Punctuation and Grammar

This section deals with word classes, punctuation, the correct tense of a word and being able to use conjunctions correctly. Let's look at some of these areas to see how you can help your child succeed.

Word classes: Making sure that your child knows how to recognise a noun, adjective, pronoun etc. is key to these questions. Here is a typical question type:

(1) Underline the nouns in these sentences.

> **Q**
> a) Brooke and Michael played in the wigwam that Louisa had erected in the back garden.
>
> b) "I had a strange dream last night that I was in love with a prince!" said the old lady.
>
> c) Rachel needs to buy some cheese, butter, bread, ham and chutney.
>
> *Answers: a) <u>Brooke</u> and <u>Michael</u> played in the <u>wigwam</u> that <u>Louisa</u> had erected in the back <u>garden</u>. b) "I had a strange <u>dream</u> last <u>night</u> that I was in <u>love</u> with a <u>prince</u>!" said the old <u>lady</u>. c) <u>Rachel</u> needs to buy some <u>cheese</u>, <u>butter</u>, <u>bread</u>, <u>ham</u> and <u>chutney</u>.*

The **skill** required in this question type is to understand which words are nouns. The **strategy** is to learn how a word is used in a text and whether it is an object, thing or naming word. One way of doing this is to ask whether a word is 'a thing' or whether it is 'a place' and if we are unsure, use another word in the phrase that we do know. For example, in question b, dream is an abstract noun as it is a thing and love is an abstract noun in this example, as it is a place. We know this because we could replace 'dream' and 'love' with a concrete noun "I had a strange pizza last night" or "I was in London with a prince".

Here is a quick reminder of the different word classes that we use in English:

WORD CLASS	DESCRIPTION	EXAMPLES
Common Noun	A thing, object	dog, book, man, tiger, house, farm
Proper Noun	Names, places, titles, days, months	Jon, Devon, York, Friday, August
Collective Noun	A word for groups of nouns	bunch, flock, herd, team, choir
Abstract Noun	A thing or place without a physical body	dream, imagination, jealousy, fun
Pronoun	This replaces the noun	she, he, it, they, we, us, our, them
Adjective	This describes the noun	short, pink, flowery, velvety, old, sad
Verb	An action or doing word	running, thinking, eating, sit, stand
Adverb	This describes the verb	quietly, deeply, speedily, hungrily
Preposition	This shows where the noun is	on, with, in, over, under, off, across
Conjunction	This joins clauses together	and, but, however, although, because
Article	This shows a specific or general noun	a, an, the

(2) **Add the correct punctuation and capital letters to the following sentence.**

Q

how many times have i told you not to use nicks mobile when were sitting around the table mum said

Answers: "How many times have I told you not to use Nick's mobile when we're sitting around the table?" Mum said.

The **skill** required in this question type is to understand the various punctuation marks that we use and how and when we apply them. One **strategy** here is to use the punctuation prompter that I use with my pupils:

Five **Q**uiet **E**lephants **I**n **C**ream **C**anoes **S**ailed **A**round **E**ngland **H**appily

F = Full Stops

Q = Question Marks

E = Exclamation Marks

These are our 'enders': these three end our sentences.

I = Inverted Commas (Speech Marks)

C = Comma

C = Colon

S = Semi colons

These are our 'breakers': They break up spoken words from non-spoken; they break up our sentences into clauses or phrases; they break up words in a list or bullet points and quotations from the text.

A = Apostrophe

E = Ellipsis

H = Hyphens

These are our 'showers': they show contraction; they show possession; they show two words compounded or they show an unfinished ending.

(3) **Underline the correct tense in these sentences.**

Q

a) I (saw, seen) you yesterday when you (was, were) at the theatre.

b) Rafael (did, done) his homework earlier and will soon be (going, gone) out.

c) They (am, are) pleased to (sing, sung) in the choir on Saturday.

Answers: a) saw, were   b) did, going   c) are, sing

Vocabulary

This section deals with singular and plural words, homophones and homonyms, antonyms and synonyms. Everything to do with extended word knowledge. Let's look at some of these areas to see how you can help your child succeed.

1 **Look at the following grid of words, then answer the questions that follow.**

recall	beat	bleach	alien	surprise
spotless	normal	pliable	remember	ordinary
flawless	alert	box	carton	foreign
whiten	desperate	dye	shock	agile

a) Find two synonyms for the word 'usual'.

b) Find two antonyms for the word 'taut'.

c) Find two synonyms for the word 'perfect'

Answers: a) normal, ordinary   b) agile, pliable   c) spotless, flawless

The **skill** here is to recognise synonyms (words most similar to) and antonyms (words most opposite to) that fulfil the questions. The **strategy** is to have a wide enough vocabulary to know the words in the grid and to know whether those words have more than one meaning. For example, the word 'box' would work equally well with 'carton' as a form of packaging, and with 'beat' as a form of fighting.

✔ HINT

Building vocabulary is critical in verbal reasoning and English exams. Encouraging a wide range of reading material is useful as reading only one author or only one genre of book will limit the exposure to words. Newspapers especially written for children are fantastic. Diaries, factual books and fictional books from old classics to modern popular books are all great for extending vocabulary in context. Themed word searches are also ideal so that a child can associate words by category.

2 **Write the correct plural form in these sentences. The singular is given in brackets.**

a) There were many _____ (reindeer) in the _____ (field).

b) They opened the _____ (box) which contained the toy _____ (lorry).

c) Our _____ (baby) will grow up to play with the other _____ (child).

Answers: a) reindeer, fields   b) boxes, lorries   c) babies, children

The **skill** required here is a thorough knowledge of the plural form of words with their associated spellings. The **strategy** is to recognise common spelling changes. The following quick reminders might help:

- Singular ending in 'y': Take off the 'y' then don't forget to add the 'i' before we add 'es', but not if it ends in 'key' so donkeys, monkeys and keys just add the 's'.

- Singular ending in 'x/ch/sh/ss/z': Add the 'es' most of the time.

- Singular ending in 'o': Either 'es' or 's' so pianos, but potatoes.

- Singular ending in 'f' or 'fe': Change the 'f' to a 'v' before adding 's' or 'es' so knives, and scarves both have 'v' instead of 'f'.

- Words that don't change: sheep, fish and deer stay exactly the same.

- Words that do change: mice = mouse, lice = louse, child = children, man = men, foot = feet.

- Weird words: ox becomes oxen.

- Most other words just add 's' but these are not 'rules' as there are so many differences.

(3) **Underline the words below that are homophones of another word not listed here.**

a) pail	sail	fail	jail	wail	tail
b) bed	red	led	wed	fed	zed
c) night	right	fight	eight	might	sight

Answers: a) pail/pale, sail/sale, wail/whale, tail/tale
b) red/read, led/lead
c) night/knight, right/write/rite, eight/ate, might/mite, sight/site

The **skill** required here is to work out which words sound like another word that has a different meaning and a different spelling. The **strategy** is to systematically work through each word and to see if there is more than one meaning of the word. It can sometimes help to sound the word out or to try thinking of as many ways of using the word, which can lead us to alternative spellings.

Word Choice

This section deals with words in context, cloze tests, anagrams or mixed up letters, crosswords, word fit and best fit. Let's look at some typical word choice questions:

(1) **Unscramble the following words so that the line of words is related to the word on the left.**

a) BIRDS	LARGINTS	PEGAIM	DRIBBLACK	DOLFINGCH
b) SPRING BULBS	LOLDIFDAF	PUTIL	YILL	SIRI
c) CLOTHING	ANGICRAD	KAJTEC	ELEEFC	TOASTICAW

Answers: a) starling, magpie, blackbird, goldfinch
b) daffodil, tulip, lily, iris   c) cardigan, jacket, fleece, waistcoat

The **skill** required here is to combine general knowledge, vocabulary and spellings. The **strategy** is to juggle the letters until the correct word is found, but there are some short cuts that can help:

- Place the letters of a word in a circle. Our eyes are used to reading in a linear way (straight line) so by mixing up the direction, our eyes can pick up patterns that would not be spotted in a linear format.

- Look for common letter groups such as 'ing', 'ight', 'fully'.

- Look at where the vowels and consonants are – there are limited groups of consonants that will fit together without a vowel in the middle and remember that in English words, an 'e' is a common ending letter, but no other vowels are common ending letters.

✅ **HINT**

Instead of always giving your child something to solve, turn it around. I ask my pupils to make 20 anagrams for me to solve in any 4 topics that they wish, and if they find a word that I cannot solve, they will win a prize (pencil toppers, scented pens and sticky lizards make a reward that most of my pupils covet!). Of course, the children are thinking of a theme, researching some words that fit the theme and then manipulating the letters to form anagrams – what more could I want in teaching the skills of anagrams by stealth!

---

(2) **Choose the word that will fit best into the space so that the sentence makes sense.**

> **Q**
>
> a) When travelling it is _____ to check tickets, passports and documents are all together.
>   a funny   b unimportant   c emergency   d vital   e exciting
>
> b) You should always wear a cycling helmet when you are on your bike to _____ your head.
>   a damage   b warm   c protect   d grip   e free
>
> c) I needed a new dress so I flicked through the _____ to see what I could buy.
>   a album   b newspaper   c journal   d catalogue   e timetable
>
> *Answers: a) d vital   b) c protect   c) d catalogue*

The **skill** here is to choose the most appropriate word to fit into the space so that the sentence makes sense. The **strategy** is to match each word against the sentence to see whether the sentence makes sense and whether it is the most appropriate word. Here are some quick tips to help with this:

- Use your knowledge of tenses to reject any words that would not fit grammatically.

- Use your knowledge of definers to reject any words that would not fit – 'an' is used before a word that begins with a vowel, 'a' or 'the' is used before a word that begins with a consonant.

- Use your knowledge of spellings to reject any words that would not fit – a moonlit NIGHT is correct but a moonlit KNIGHT will never be correct so watch that spellings don't trip you up!

- Use your knowledge of vocabulary to reject any words that would not fit – if more than one word has the same meaning, then neither of them will fit so you can probably reject them both.

(3) **Find one word that will fit into the space that makes sense of the sentence.**

> **Q**
> a) He had to _____ his white shirt to turn it dark blue.
>
> b) When she began to use a fountain pen, she always had _____ on her fingers.
>
> c) The five little _____ followed the swan as she led her babies to the water's edge.
>
> *Answers: a) dye   b) ink   c) cygnets*

The **skill** required here is to find the one word that will fit into the space using the clues from the text. The **strategy** is to think of what word is needed, to think of all possible words that would fit into the space to make sense and then to reject each one until only one logical word remains. Here is an example of this strategy with question a.

He had to ????? his white shirt to turn it dark blue.

Clues: what turns something dark blue? Blue paint, ink, nail varnish, coloured hairspray, blue pop, dye...

Nail varnish? No – it would take lots of bottles to turn a shirt blue

Ink? This does stain things but it is not the easiest way of turning a whole white shirt blue

Blue paint? Hmm, not really unless you painted it all – this is unlikely

Which is likely to turn a white shirt blue?

Blue pop? – this is blue but it wouldn't turn a white shirt dark blue.

Coloured hairspray? – this would turn hair blue, but not really a white shirt

Dye? Yes this would turn a white shirt blue

All of these question types are explained in further detail in *Bond How To Do 11⁺ English*, which can be bought or ordered from most bookshops. (See Appendix B for details.)

Maths

11^+ maths tests cover a spectrum of maths principles and concepts. They examine how effectively a child can understand and manipulate numbers. 11^+ maths can be divided into four main sections: Graphic Data, Shape and Size, Number Equations and Number Logic.

Graphic Data:
- Use graphs, charts, tables and decision trees
- Understand coordinates and compass points
- Work with scale and dimension
- Understand conversions

Shape and Size:
- Recognise shape transformations
- Understand vertices, faces and edges
- Solve perimeter, area and volume
- Understand angles

Maths Question Types

Number Equations:
- Use division, multiplication, addition and subtraction
- Understand multiples and factors
- Understand fractions, decimals and percentages
- Use prime, square and cube numbers

Number Logic
- Use negative and positive numbers
- Understand number lines
- Make number squares
- Understand probability and ratio
- Use mean, mode, median and range
- Understand algebra

Let's have a look in more detail at each section and understand how you can help your child succeed at maths.

Graphic Data

This section covers the use of coordinates, compass points and the elements of scale and dimension. Can your child understand conversions? Can they use decision trees and read tables, graphs and charts? Typical questions in the area of graphic data include the following.

	High St	Wood End	Market	Church	Terminus
Bus A	09:14	09:20	09:50	10:03	10:15
Bus B	10:00	10:06		10:30	10:42
Bus C	11:20	11:26	11:52		12:10

(1) Look at the timetable above and then complete the following questions:

Q
a) How long does Bus A take to get from High St to the Terminus?

b) How long does it take from the Church to the Terminus?

c) What is the quickest time from Wood End to the Market?

Answers: a) 1 hr 1 minute   b) 12 minutes   c) 26 minutes

The **skill** required is to make deductions from the data given and a general awareness of subtraction and addition is also useful. The **strategy** needed is to look at what the question is actually asking. For example, in question c, your child is trying to find the quickest time from one place to another so it is not sufficient to use any bus, but to make comparisons with one against another.

(2) Look at this grid and answer the following questions.

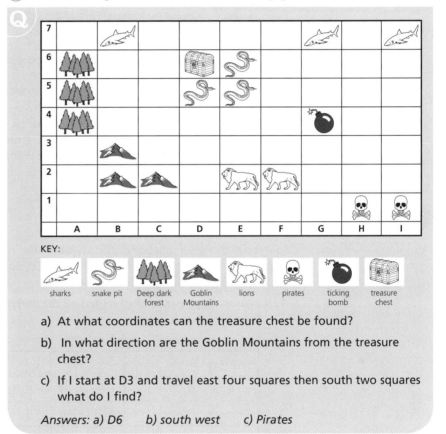

a) At what coordinates can the treasure chest be found?

b) In what direction are the Goblin Mountains from the treasure chest?

c) If I start at D3 and travel east four squares then south two squares what do I find?

Answers: a) D6   b) south west   c) Pirates

The **skill** here is to recognise how the grid and coordinates work and where the compass points are. The **strategy** needed is for your child to understand that each coordinate is mapping an item. Knowing how to relate the compass point with the grid and key, and understanding that coordinates are read across the horizontal and then down the vertical, means information can be retrieved accurately and quickly.

(3) We showed Year 4, Year 5 and Year 6 classes some pictures of baby animals and asked the children which baby animal looked the cutest. Look at the following table then answer the questions that follow.

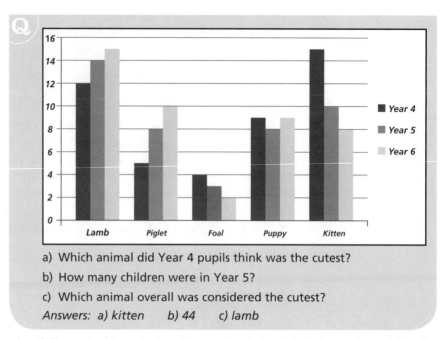

a) Which animal did Year 4 pupils think was the cutest?

b) How many children were in Year 5?

c) Which animal overall was considered the cutest?

Answers: a) kitten   b) 44   c) lamb

The **skill** required here is the ability to find the right information within the table that will answer the questions. The **strategy** needed is to understand how these charts work so that a child is clear which column shows which information, to understand how the numbers on the left represent the number of pupils asked and that each group of three columns represent the animals shown.

Shape and Size

This section looks at shape transformations, the various parts of a 3D shape, perimeter, area and volume and angles. Here are some typical shape and size questions:

(1) **Look at shape A and then underline the correct answer in the statements that follow.**

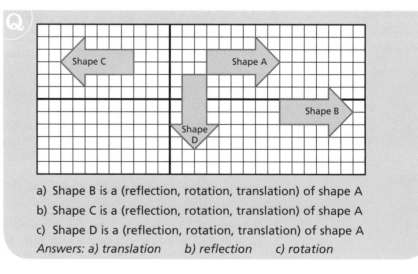

a) Shape B is a (reflection, rotation, translation) of shape A

b) Shape C is a (reflection, rotation, translation) of shape A

c) Shape D is a (reflection, rotation, translation) of shape A

Answers: a) translation   b) reflection   c) rotation

The **skill** required is to recognise how a shape has been transformed. The **strategy** needed is to understand how a shape can be transformed. One method of remembering the transformations is as follows:

Translate = slide – it can only move about, it cannot spin or flip over. (It has 'sl' in it for 'slide')

Rotate = spin around – it can only spin, not slide or flip

Reflect = flip over – it can only be a symmetrical reflection, it cannot slide or spin about. *(We see our **reflection** in a mirror so we see our shape flipped over in a mirror line.)*

(2) **Look at the following shapes, then solve the area/perimeter/volume questions.**

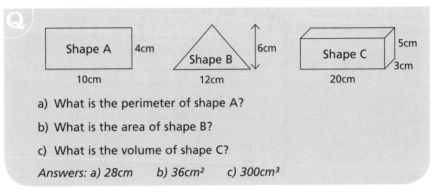

a) What is the perimeter of shape A?

b) What is the area of shape B?

c) What is the volume of shape C?

Answers: a) 28cm   b) 36cm²   c) 300cm³

The **skill** required is to understand how to solve a perimeter, area and volume of various shapes. The **strategy** needed is to remember how we find the elements of a shape. Here is a quick reminder of the formulas needed:

- To find an area of a square and rectangle we multiply the length by the height.
- To find an area of a triangle we multiply the length by the height and then divide by two.
- To find a perimeter of a shape, we add up all of the outside edges.
- To find the volume of a shape we multiply the length by the height by the depth.

(3) **In the parallelogram below, angle x measures 70°. What is the size of angle y?**

Answer: 110°

The **skill** required is a knowledge of shapes, angles and parallel lines. The **strategy** needed is to recognise which shapes have parallel lines and which do not. Here is a quick reminder to help us with angles:

- There are 360° in a full turn (one circle)
- There are 180° in a half turn (one semicircle – this makes a straight line)

- There are 90° in a quarter turn (one quarter – this makes a right angle)
- There are 360° in a four sided shape
- There are 180° in a triangle
- Opposite angles of a square, rectangle, rhombus and parallelogram are equal

Now if we look back at Q3, we can see that there is a straight line with angle 'x' measuring 70°. If we subtract 70 from 180 (angle 'x' taken from the straight line) we are left with 110°.

We know that opposite angles of a parallelogram are equal so we know that angle 'y' is 110°.

> ✓ **HINT**
>
> *To help your child, make sure that they know the following terms and methods:*
> - *What an acute angle, obtuse angle, right angle and reflex angle is*
> - *How many degrees are in a circle, straight line, rectangle and triangle*
> - *How to find the area of a rectangle and triangle*
> - *How to find the perimeter of a shape*
> - *How to find the volume of a cuboid*
> - *What the different forms of transformation are*
> - *What the four averages are*
> - *How to add, subtract, multiply and divide*

Number Equations

This section looks at the four basic number operators: multiplication, division, subtraction and addition. It looks at multiples and factors, understanding fractions, decimals and percentages and prime, square and cubed numbers. Let's have a look at some typical number equation questions.

(1) **Read the following information and then solve the problem.**

> **Q**
>
> Pham Quang goes to Scouts, (£1.50 a week), plays in the orchestra, (£2.00 a week), plays football twice a week, (£2.50 each time), goes to Chinese school, (£24.80 every four weeks) and he goes to drama, (£3.00 a week).
>
> a) What is the total cost for Pham Quang each week?
>
> b) If Pham Quang does these activities for 46 weeks of the year, how much would it cost at the end of the year?
>
> c) If Pham Quang pays for the year in advance, he will get a reduction of 10%. How much would he pay now for the year?
>
> *Answers: a) £17.70   b) £814.20   c) £732.78*

The **skill** here is the ability to perform addition, division, subtraction and multiplication as well as understanding percentages. The **strategy** is to break this question down into manageable chunks. Encourage your child to set out the initial sums into an easy to read format and then to work out each calculation like this:

STEP a:		STEP b:	STEP c:	
Scouts	£ 1.50	17.70 ×	£ 814.20	10% = £81.42
Orchestra	£ 2.00	46		
Football x 2	£ 5.00	**£ 814.20**		
Chinese School ÷ 4	£ 6.20		£ 814.20	
Drama	£ 3.00		£ 81.42 –	
TOTAL	**£ 17.70**		**£ 732.78**	

(2) **Find the following Lowest Common Multiples (LCM) and Highest Common Factors (HCF).**

Q
  a) The LCM of 5 and 6

  b) The HCF of 20 and 50

  c) The LCM of 2, 3 and 4

Answers: a) 30   b) 10   c) 12

The **skill** required here is to find one number that fulfils the criteria for the numbers given. The **strategy** is to work methodically through the LCMs/HCFs. Remember that a common multiple is just the multiplication table until you find the lowest match. With the common factor, it is all of the numbers that fit into the number until you find the highest number that matches, like this:

LCM of 5 = 5, 10, 15, 20, 25, **30**   LCM of 6 = 6, 12, 18, 24, **30**

HCF of 20 = 1, 2, 4, 5, **10**, 20   HCF of 50 = 1, 2, 5, **10**, 25, 50

(3) **Solve the following equations.**

Q
  a) What is 40% of 200?

  b) What is $\frac{3}{4}$ of 36?

  c) What is 0.20 of 60?

Answers: a) 80   b) 27   c) 12

The **skill** here is to be able to work comfortably with percentages, fractions and decimals. The **strategy** is to remember how we solve these types of equations. Here is a useful list of formula that can help us:

To Find a Percentage of a Number:
Divide the number by 100 and multiply by the percentage.
E.g. 40% of 200 is: 200 ÷ 100 = 2   2 × 40 = 80

To Find a Fraction of a Number:
Divide the number by the denominator (the bottom number) and multiply by the top number.
E.g. $\frac{3}{4}$ of 36 is: 36 ÷ 4 = 9   9 × 3 = 27

To Find a Decimal of a Number:
Divide the number by 100 and multiply by the decimal number after the decimal point.
E.g. 0.20 of 60 is: 60 ÷ 100 = 0.6   0.6 × 20 = 12

This section looks at number lines, number squares, probability, ratio, the four averages, positive and negative numbers and algebra. Let's look at some typical number logic questions.

(1) **All of the children in Year 6 have sat an English test and here are their results.**

Class 6A	20	18	14	15	22	19	15	17	12	9
Class 6B	15	16	18	18	20	24	19	13	12	15
Class 6C	25	23	24	21	24	20	19	24	22	16

a) What is the range for class 6A?

b) What is the mean for class 6B?

c) What is the mode for class 6C?

Answers: a) 13   b) 17   c) 24

The **skill** required for this question is to apply the correct average to the number set to solve the problems. The **strategy** is to work systematically remembering which average is which. Here is a quick way of recalling the averages:

Range: Subtract the smallest number from the biggest number.
For example in question a: $22 - 9 = 13$

Mean: Add all of the numbers together, then divide them all up by the number of numbers.
For example in question b:
$(15 + 16 + 18 + 18 + 20 + 24 + 19 + 13 + 12 + 15) \div 10 = 17$

Mode: The most common number.
For example in question c:
$1 \times 25, 1 \times 23, \mathbf{3 \times 24}, 1 \times 21, 1 \times 20, 1 \times 19, 1 \times 22, 1 \times 16 = 24$

Median: To solve the median we put the numbers in order, smallest to largest, then we choose the middle number or, if there are two middle numbers, we choose the halfway point between the two.
For example, if we wanted the median for 6A we would do the following:
20, 18, 14, 15, 22, 19, 15, 17, 12, 9 = 9, 12, 14, 15, **15, 17**, 18, 19, 20, 22
The median = **16**

(2) **Complete the grid:**

	3 + x	5 – x	7x	12 ÷ x	x + x + x
x = 2					
x = 3					

Answers:

	3 + x	5 – x	7x	12 ÷ x	x + x + x
x = 2	5	3	14	6	6
x = 3	6	2	21	4	9

The **skill** required here is a recognition of an equation where 'x' represents a given number and to carry out calculations using 'x =' to complete a grid. The **strategy** is first to understand the grid and then to replace x with the numbers given in each equation. Encourage your child to use a logical thinking pattern to fulfil each criterion like this:

If $x = 2$, then $3 + x$ means $3 + 2 = 5$ If $x = 2$, then $7x$ means $7 \times 2 = \mathbf{14}$
If $x = 3$, then $3 + x$ means $3 + 3 = \mathbf{6}$ If $x = 3$, then $7x$ means $7 \times 3 = \mathbf{21}$

(**3**) What are the missing numbers in these number squares?

Q

4		2
	5	
8	1	6

	18	
6	10	14
16		12

6	18	21
12	24	9

Answers

4	9	2
3	5	7
8	1	6

8	18	4
6	10	14
16	2	12

27	3	15
6	18	21
12	24	9

The **skill** with number squares is to understand how they work and to calculate the correct numbers. The **strategy** is to recognise that in a number square, every row – horizontal, vertical and diagonal – will all add up to the same number. The key is finding the one full row and once we have added that row up, we can then work out the other calculations.

All of the questions types are explained in further detail in *Bond How to Do 11⁺ Maths*, which can be bought or ordered from most bookshops. (See Appendix B for details.)

11⁺ Frequently Asked Questions...

About My Child

 My child is bright at many subjects, but struggles at maths/English – what can I do to help them?

The Bond Placement Tests in this book will help to identify where the problem areas are and will suggest which books and resources that your child needs to strengthen a weak area. Each book in the series is carefully graded to ensure steady progress is made and the answer booklets make it easy for parents to check accuracy.

 My child has dyslexia / specific learning difficulties / specific needs, can they still pass the 11⁺ exam?

Individual schools should all have a policy on fair examination opportunities for all children. The test papers and test environment should cater for your child whether it is for large print, extra time or whatever your child needs to be given a fair attempt at the paper, but the best advice is to contact the school or the LEA and to ask what is available for your child. Make sure you notify schools in advance so that they have time to prepare.

 My child was ill for their SATs and we don't know what level they are at. What should we do?

Have a word with your child's class teacher and see what level they think your child is working at. The different methods of assessing your child may not be complete, but as long as you have at least the results from the Bond Placement Tests plus one other area of comparison (a reading age or school/class teacher report would be especially useful) you should be able to gain some idea of where you child is up to. Some schools prefer not to inform parents of where their child is up to in their SATs, so again, use the results from the Bond Placement Tests plus at least one other form of assessment.

 My child was born in August, is it fair that they are tested with children almost a year older?

Many schools provide a standardised system of testing so that children are competing on an equal level. This means that the scores for the exam, alongside scores for the date of birth are used to provide a final result. It is also true that a child in Year 5, whether born in September or the following August, have all followed exactly the same curriculum so they are not necessarily disadvantaged by their birth month.

Q My child is bright and capable, but they are very slow to work questions out. Does this mean that they are going to fail the 11+?

The Bond system uses timed papers and following the books will ensure that your child becomes used to working within a time frame. The Bond 10 Minute Tests series can be especially useful in building time because a quick enough processing speed is important in the exam. There are some ideas for improving timing and technique in this book so have a go with some of them and see how your child responds. I've found that many 'slow' children are actually perfectionists who cannot bear to miss out a question that they are struggling with or they feel the need to double and treble check every question. Reassure your child that learning is a fun process and that making a mistake is part of education and to be expected and welcomed. There are many children who are reprimanded for making mistakes, for not focusing fully or for making 'silly' mistakes and in this instance, it is understandable that no answer would seem better than a punishable one.

Q I have a child who makes 'silly' mistakes because she won't focus and it drives me mad when she keeps making them. What can I do to stop her from failing the 11+?

As a teacher, I have rarely seen a child gain top marks out of fear. I have seen children extremely upset when they have their papers marked because they are worried about letting their parents down or because of their own frustration at losing marks. Of course accuracy is important and ensuring basic skills are strong will help in this. To this end, knowing times tables, knowing how to multiple and divide, knowing spelling rules etc. are all recommended but changing a child from a daydreamer into a calculating machine is another matter. In tutoring, I have found the most success by reassuring a child that they are not 'wrong' or have 'a problem' that needs sorting, but rather they have a toolbox of skills of which they should feel proud. They need to use the skills they already have and become open to new skills that are unfamiliar at first, but can become more familiar and useful in time.

It might mean taking baby steps that build towards a skill. For example, one girl always missed out questions because her eyes would dart around the page. At the end of each page, we tried to encourage her to place a tick next to each question to show that she had answered it. This was time consuming at first, but it dealt with the problem as she then easily found all of the questions that she had missed out. Another child would always begin daydreaming and lose track of time when left to his own devices, so we tried using an alarm clock set in short blocks of time. He had to reach the end of the section before the alarm went off and, very slowly, we began increasing the length of sections between the alarm sounding.

This type of stepped approach can be frustrating as it is a slow process, but if the end result works and your child learns new skills that they will use throughout their life, it is so rewarding and yes, both of these children passed the 11+ exam and went off to their first choice school happy and contented with their new found skills. Frustration from you and your child is normal, but working on the new skill of concentrated focus makes it easier to understand that it is not your child's fault if they find this skill difficult. They are not 'misbehaving', as losing focus is not something that they can control, but it is a skill that can be worked on and improved and it is such a worthwhile skill to gain.

 My child is top of the year, but I've just found out that their school is not an academic school. How can I judge how bright my child really is?

This is one of the reasons why the SATs tests were brought in to create parity. The Bond Placement Tests in the middle of this book are there to try and assess your child against a standard and to find out where your child is in terms of the 11+ needs and requirements.

 My child has done the placement tests, but they are only average. Is it possible for them to pass the 11+?

This depends upon how much time you have before the exam, how much work there is to cover before the exam, how motivated your child and you are, and crucially, what your child's potential is. I have assessed some pupils who have been well below average and my suggestion has been to work on key skill areas and then reassess to see how much progress has been made. One girl in particular scored well below average in both maths and English and she was sitting an exam that needed maths, English and verbal reasoning. She was super motivated and obviously had the potential as she ended up scoring extremely highly with a score of 100% in her maths paper. This is because some children in school are not reaching their full potential for whatever reason, so with some concentrated work on the basics, a child can come on a huge amount. There will also be some children who are working below, or at, national average and they are already reaching their full potential. In this instance it would not be possible for them to pass the 11+. Timing is also critical as the longer you have, the more opportunity there will be for your child to make improvements. The plan in this book will help with this.

 My child is struggling with 11+ material, how can I tell them they are not good enough for the 11+?

It is worth looking at where they are struggling. Is it technique based, remembering what to do, a lack of word knowledge, an inability to work in time? If it is technique based, try using the *How To Do* 11+ books or perhaps find a tutor for a lesson or two. If it is remembering, take some time to consolidate the techniques and perhaps try one of the Bond books at the same level to get more used to these skills. The *Stretch Practice* series and *Up To Speed Practice* series can be useful as can the 10 Minute Tests series. It might be worth moving a step backwards and try the lower age book to build confidence and remembrance. If your child is struggling with timing, there is further information in this book on some techniques to try. Ultimately if your child is struggling too much and you have decided to not sit the 11+ I have found the following five points useful:

1) Explain that there is a best school for everyone and a selective school is not 'the best' school; it is the best school for some people just as there is a best school for your child.

2) Empower them by discussing why you think it best not to do the 11+ and ask for their view so that they feel as though they have contributed to the decision to stop and understand the reasons why.

3) Tell your child that you are proud of them for having a go at such a tricky challenge.

4) Reassure them that they are not 'a numpty', but this particular 11+ test doesn't play to their strengths.

5) Remind them of the skills that they are great at (sport, music, dancing, friendliness, kindness, creativity etc.)

 Is there any benefit in following the Bond system if I am not putting my child in for the 11+?

The English and maths books will definitely help your child with their numeracy and literacy as they can strengthen skills that the SATs are based on and that fulfils the National Curriculum. Most of my pupils like to continue with the Bond system for the remainder of their Year 6 as it allows them to consolidate their literacy and numeracy skills. In terms of the verbal and non-verbal reasoning, they can help to develop logical thinking and the verbal reasoning builds great vocabulary so they will help with transferable skills, but they won't directly help with the school curriculum.

About Schools

 Academies, free schools, comprehensive schools, grammar schools, private schools – what is the difference and which have an 11+ exam?

There is so much confusion about these terms. In the 1990s some failing schools were entitled to apply for academy status with the aim of raising their standards. These schools were state managed and were called 'sponsored academies'. Admission to these schools was open and free to all. A free school is a new school that has to be open to all children, again with an inclusive admissions policy. A comprehensive school is a state-maintained (free) school that is open to all children. A grammar school is often state-maintained (free), but has a selection process – an 11+ exam. Some grammar schools are fee-paying. In 2010, a new academy status was brought in to allow the top achieving schools, many of them grammar schools, to become more independent in areas such as budget, funding and staffing. Some of these schools do use an 11+ entrance exam. A private school or public school education is one that is paid for and most of these schools have some form of selection process. There are resources that can help with the various schools in your area, those that are free and fee paying. See Appendix B for further information.

 How fierce is competition for the 11+?

There are usually more pupils applying for grammar schools than there are places available and so competition can be fierce. When a school has an admissions policy based on the 11+ results only, those with the highest results take the places. Parents can now 'choose' which school their child goes to, even if the school is out of the catchment area, but the right to choose a school is really a right to express a preference, as there is no guarantee that a school place will be made available to your child. When a school is under subscribed, it will always be easier to be offered a place and when a school is over subscribed, the competition becomes greater. Now that pupils can take the exam and find out the results before they apply for a school, the competition in some LEAs is greater than ever.

Q Why is it so hard to find out information about the 11+?

Since the 1970s there has been a political move away from selective school processes to state school comprehensive systems. For this reason, fewer schools and LEAs are using the 11+ selection system. Many schools within 11+ LEAs are reluctant to prepare for the 11+ and in some cases they would prefer to give the minimum amount of information to parents. Political perspectives change through public opinion and the political party of the day, but selective schools are as desirable as ever.

Q Can I bypass the exam and pay for a place?

If the school you are applying for is based totally on academic admission, then no, you could offer the moon on a stick and they won't accept your child. You will be able to find out in the school admissions policy whether places are offered based on academic admission only.

Q I already have a child in the school and I know the head teacher socially, so will this make a difference?

Not if the school is based totally on academic admission. If the school lists siblings as a criteria then it may be beneficial, but in many cases this will only be relevant at an appeal so read the admissions information carefully to understand how your school selects pupils. In terms of knowing the head teacher, in many state-funded schools, it is the LEA who makes the decisions on school places based purely on academic score and your head teacher may have no say in the matter unless it goes to appeal and even then, the LEA may have the final decision.

Q How many schools can my child apply for?

Your child can sit the 11+ in their primary school for a state-funded grammar and then as many 11+ exams for private schools as you wish. If your school is not in an 11+ LEA you could sit several 11+ exams in selective schools. In a state-funded grammar school, most parents will know the results before they apply for schools, but even in these cases, always use the full quota of schools that you can, as an appeal can only be placed for schools that are on the school preference form. I know of a parent putting the same one grammar school for all of their choices so that the school knew that they were serious about that school. The school was over subscribed and as there were no other schools listed they were given the local comprehensive school that they did not want. Unfortunately the appeal process was difficult as no other schools were offered as a preference so the other schools that the parents would have considered were now full. Passing the exam does not guarantee being offered a place so take the school preference form seriously and make sure you put down schools that you would want.

About the 11+ Exam and Preparation for it

 How is the 11+ exam different from other school exams?

National exams such as SATs are part of the government framework for education. GCSEs are a cornerstone of secondary school learning and although not compulsory, they are internationally recognised qualifications that are offered in most schools. The 11+ exam is part of the secondary school selection process for schools that select potential pupils by academic ability.

 Surely a child has all they need in schools. Why would a bright child need extra help?

The English and maths element of the 11+ should follow the syllabus used in schools, but verbal and non-verbal reasoning are not taught in state schools. Giving your child a verbal or non-verbal reasoning exam is similar to an adult with no linguistic skills taking a paper written in a foreign language. Preparing your child for any exam is natural. We would revise for any exam in order to do our best, so I would not consider revision for the 11+ as innately wrong, nor is solid teaching of knowledge and skills, as long as this is balanced alongside school-based homework and other extra-curricular activities.

 How much tutoring is okay and how much is 'wrong'?

My personal view is simply that there are many perspectives, but I don't have a problem teaching a child a skill that they did not know before. Revising is to practise these skills so that they become known and understood fully. Revising is also working to time which can help in any timed exam. I would encourage any child to reach their full potential and in doing so I teach maths, English, verbal and non-verbal reasoning as a wide, rich, broad syllabus that develop strong skills that a child can use throughout their life. I will also encourage them to revise and consolidate by practising their new found skills, but endlessly practising the same exam paper without the skills behind it is not something that I would recommend. There will always be parents who have their child tutored and this is the system of selective education that we are a part of whether we like it or not. As parents and teachers, we know our children and have a responsibility to ensure that the decisions we make are the best for our child and that the workload we put them under is never unreasonable. If a child is struggling at 11+ level to get into a school, are you prepared to either provide tutors every week through secondary school just to keep them at the school or have the heartbreaking decision of withdrawing your child from a school where they cannot cope?

Is it possible to prepare a child for a 'tutor-proof' CEM style exam?

It is possible to give children a range of skills and techniques to deepen their understanding for any exam. My personal view is that the CEM style exam supports my feelings about children having real learning and not just jumping through an exam paper hoop without real knowledge. It is understandable for a parent to grab a pack of papers and to feverishly push their child through them repeatedly until the pass mark is reached, but this really isn't the best way for a child to learn. The skills needed for any 11⁺ exam is to have thorough knowledge of numeracy and literacy skills, a wide ranging vocabulary and the ability to think logically and systematically. There is plenty of material and resources to help children to do this and to give them the best possible opportunity of succeeding in any 11⁺ exam. CEM do not recognise nor recommend any range of books or papers so there will only be CEM 'style' resources available. The Bond CEM Assessment Papers and *How To Do* books provide help and practice. Appendix B has more information on this.

Q Can past papers be bought for practice?

For the LEAs who commission an exam board to write the 11⁺ paper, it is not usually possible to beg, borrow or steal past exam papers. What you can get hold of are general example papers written by the exam boards, which can be bought from bookshops. For those schools that set their own papers, they will often send out copies of past papers, as will schools that sit the CEE.

Q Can my child retake the 11⁺ if they fail it?

No – the 11⁺ exam is a one attempt only paper. If you are applying for numerous schools or schools out of an area, there may well be lots of 11⁺ exams for your child to sit, but no 11⁺ paper can be repeated. Sometimes a child may fail the 11⁺ but in a year or two, would like to try again and in these instances, a 12⁺ or 13⁺ paper may be offered. Usually, if this is offered, it is conditional upon a place being available in the school year. In some schools, especially some of the most selective schools where entry to senior school is at Year 7 or Year 9, if an 11⁺ is failed, it is not possible for a child to be entered into a 13⁺ exam. It is worth checking this out beforehand as in some schools, an 11⁺ exam might be more or less advantageous than sitting the 13⁺.

Q Will my child also need to sit an interview in addition to the 11⁺ exam?

It depends upon the admissions policy. Most state-funded grammar schools have no interview but many of the fee-paying schools will have an interview. If your child is invited for an interview, they may be asked to bring along schoolbooks and sometimes certificates or awards from 'out of school' activities. This needs to be selective so do include your child's latest music, dance, sporting award or newspaper cuttings of events your child has taken part in, but don't take along every piece of artwork your child has created, or certificates older than a couple of years. (You are rightly proud of their 'Little Ducklings Pre-School Swimming Certificate for Improvement', but a secondary school will be more impressed to see that your child has been swimming on a regular basis for nine years, as this shows dedication and perseverance.) In some of the top fee-paying schools, your child may be asked about subjects that they have studied in school, something topical in the news or to interpret a piece of artwork.

Q **How can my child prepare for an interview?**

Encourage your child to express their ideas clearly and confidently. This skill can be helped through your child joining a debating society, a drama class or by volunteering for presentations in school. The interviewer is looking for pupils who will best suit their school environment. Read the school prospectus to see what they value. Do they highlight sports, music, drama, travel, religion? How well does your child meet these values? Look at how their hobbies and interest can strengthen transferable skills, for example, 'Playing the flute in the orchestra has helped me to be confident' or 'Playing ice-hockey has helped me to work effectively in a team".

Q **There are so many 11⁺ books and papers in the shops and online. How do I know what to buy?**

I know how terrifying it all seems. First of all it is vital to know your school. What exam subject does it use? What date is your 11⁺ exam? Which exam board creates the papers? These are key questions for the following reasons: your school might only test one subject or it might test in all four subjects. It might use a standard format, or it might use a multiple choice format. Your school might use a GL assessment or a CEM style assessment and there are books, resources and materials for every configuration so don't panic. Check your schools and later on in the book, there will be the opportunity to plan whatever you need.

Q **Do I have to get a tutor for the 11⁺?**

No! There is sufficient material and resources out there to support your child. Some parents pay for a tutor for many years to prepare their child, other parents pay for one or two sessions of tutoring to strengthen specific skills or to book in a 'mock test' and many parents prepare their child without using any tutor at all. Having a tutor does not guarantee a child will pass and not having a tutor does not mean that your child will fail. You know your child, yourself and your budget so use this as a guide. This book will help in making your decision and finding the best system for you and your child.

Q **Is it going to cost a lot of money to sit the 11⁺ exam?**

No! It is all relative, but so many parents purchase every single book and paper with 11⁺ written on it and then their poor child drowns in a sea of confusion that is likely to do more harm than good. There are some free resources out there and some extremely expensive ones. Some parents pay for a tutor, some use a tutoring system, some use a *How To Do* range of books and work alongside their child. Some websites have fabulous free resources and there are apps and games to offer maximum support for minimal cost, so please don't feel as though your child is unable to sit the 11⁺ exam because of finance. In our plans, we even use a costing system to help you budget for the 11⁺ beforehand.

Q **Why is the Bond series preferable to other resources?**

There are many books and resources, some are excellent and some are awful. I am unaware of any books or paper out there that I haven't tried and I keep up to date with every new resource. I still wholeheartedly prefer Bond. I began using the Bond system well before I started writing for them and that is why I write for Bond. My reasons for using them are that they are systematic, thorough, affordable and supportive and I achieve great success for my pupils using Bond. It is not the only resource that I use (Appendix B lists other resources), but it provides the majority of what I use. I like the chart in the back that allows children, parents and myself to track how a child is progressing and the layout is straightforward and not distracting with cartoons or boxes. The main huge advantage though, is with consolidation. If a child has one long paper on a topic, they cover that topic and practise it. They then turn over and learn a new topic. By the end of the book, a child has covered everything, but can remember nothing as the techniques are not consolidated. The Bond book mixes up the topics on every paper so that children practise the skills and consolidate them. The books don't have gimmicks, stars, stickers or cartoons but they offer a solid, thorough, complete learning programme that provides excellent value for money.

What About the Type of Test?

At the time of writing, there are three main styles of 11⁺ testing and any one, or a mixture, may be chosen by a school, hence the need for checking which examination provider your school chooses:

1) Set format of limited question types. Test providers such as GL Assessment (used to be referred to as NFER), the CEA and Moray House provide 11⁺ tests in separate test areas in standard and/or multiple choice formats. They use a bank of test questions ensuring that questions are changed year by year, but there are a set number of question types used and the technique required to answer these question types can be learnt. The exam requires strong vocabulary, logic, maths skills and spellings so strengthening these areas will underpin the exam. There are many packs of 11⁺ papers that can be bought, alongside books that provide help for these exams.

   "I had two mock papers, a week apart and then two real papers, a week apart. Each exam lasted 50 minutes and I had 80 questions to answer all in multiple choice format. Between all four papers, there was every style of question that I had covered in my Bond books and papers. I felt confident in my exams as there was nothing that I hadn't been prepared for. I was so pleased that I had prepared in advance so that there were no surprises on the day."

2) Unknown format of wide ranging question types. Test provider CEM (University of Durham) uses a less prescriptive test so that it is much harder to predict the question types and because there is no set technique for each question type, the CEM exam is considered 'tutor-proof' and fairer. The emphasis on wide ranging skills in maths, vocabulary, comprehension and spellings is perhaps more based on school literacy and numeracy and it would be wonderful if all children could be treated equally so that no parent has to pay for additional tuition for their child. It is inevitable though, that many

parents will just organise additional English and maths for their child and the additional emphasis on vocabulary and spellings may well discriminate against children who have not been exposed to a wide range of vocabulary, rather than making it fairer on children who have not been tutored. The areas of testing are more mixed with verbal reasoning and English as one paper and non-verbal reasoning and maths as another paper. There are some packs of 11+ papers that can be bought alongside books that provide help for strengthening skills that are likely to be tested in these exams. Strengthening English, comprehension, vocabulary and spellings and having secure maths skills is key to the CEM.

"There was a lot more time pressure as there were a lot of questions to answer in the time. There were cloze tests, a comprehension and lots of synonyms and antonyms in the first paper. We then had a short break followed by the second paper which was a mixture of maths and NVR. Each paper was only 45 minutes long. I needed quick maths skills as well as worded maths problems. I couldn't believe it was all over on one day, but I was glad that we had done lots of work on the basics as the format of the question doesn't really matter as long as you know how to answer it. There was an example given for each question type and we had a practice attempt for the question before we answered the rest of the section."

3) Style specific to a school or consortium. Some schools or consortiums prepare their own entrance tests and may include a mix of multiple choice and standard format and might include a separate paper as a written composition or as problem solving. Many schools and consortiums provide test papers for pupils, but many of the main books and papers can also be used to build the skills required for these exams. Again, it is strong literacy and numeracy skills that will be useful skills, in addition to comprehension, writing and problem solving.

"There were a lot of maths questions to complete in the time allowed and they were challenging. The problem solving was also tricky, but I liked the written test as I could choose from three titles. The comprehension was not very long, but it was quite difficult and the English grammar paper was multiple choice with lots of spellings and punctuation questions. I was pleased that the tests were spread over two days, but I would have liked a mock exam to have known what to expect on the day."

Checklist for Step 1 Success

- ☐ I know what the 11+ test is
- ☐ I know when my LEA 11+ test is and what is tested
- ☐ I understand what verbal reasoning is about
- ☐ I understand what non-verbal reasoning is about
- ☐ I understand what English is about
- ☐ I understand what maths is about
- ☐ I'm ready to assess my child
- ☐ My thoughts, feelings, questions and notes are:

....

....

....

....

....

....

....

....

....

....

....

....

....

....

....

STEP 2

Assess Your Child

- ○ Build up a Picture of Your Child's Ability
- ○ Bond Placement Tests
- ○ Find the Spelling Age
- ○ Record the Results
- ○ Checklist for Step 2 Success

◄ Doesn't every parent think that their own child is a genius? Mine is probably average. ►

◄ *I don't want my child to be set up for a failure. How can I protect them?* ►

◄ All of her friends are going to grammar school and I don't want her to miss out on the opportunity, but I don't want her to struggle. What can I do? ►

◄ *How can I really tell how bright my child really is? I wish there was another way of assessing them so that we can decide which school is best for him.* ►

◄ When I asked the school if my child was suitable for taking the 11+ the teacher said that she didn't believe in the 11+ and would therefore refuse to answer the question. ►

◄ *My daughter goes to a village school. She is top of her year, but her class is tiny. How can I judge how bright she is compared to other children of her age?* ►

◄ How can I decide whether it is worth us pursuing the 11+ route into secondary school? ►

◄ *The class teacher thinks that my son is academically poor, but I am sure that he is far more capable. Can I assess his ability without going through the school?* ►

◄ My child has specific learning difficulties, but she is bright in many ways. Could she be bright enough for the 11+? ►

Build Up a Picture of Your Child's Ability

Deciding whether to enter your child for the 11+ exam can be a difficult decision. This will be made much easier when you are fully informed of your child's progress and ability. Here are some key sources of information to gather that will help with your decision-making process:

SATs / CATs / PIEs / PIMs:

How did your child perform in their KS1 SATs test? What are their predicted results for KS2 SATs at the end of Year 6? Has your school used CAT tests, end of year exams, PIEs and PIMs and if so, how has your child performed in these?

Reading and Spelling Age:

Is your child advanced in their reading and spelling? Are they proficient at reading for understanding? Have they gained a wide range of vocabulary? Do they understand spelling strings and spelling rules? Are they interested in word games?

School Report:

What is the assessment of your child's class teacher? Is your child above average in their class? Does the class teacher feel that grammar school is the best education for your child? If not, why?

Assess Your Child For The 11+

Bond Placement Tests:

Look at the results from the Bond Placement Tests, which will give an indication of where your child is up to at present. Is there sufficient time for your child to work through to the 11+ level books? Does your child have a spelling age and a reading age that is at least equal to their real age?

General Knowledge:

Does your child enjoy finding out factual information? How good are they at remembering and recalling facts and figures? Do they enjoy watching science, history and geography programmes? Do they enjoy children's encyclopaedias? Do they enjoy researching for school projects on new topics?

Logic Games:

Does your child perform well at crosswords, word searches, logic games or quizzes? Do they enjoy computer or console games that require tactical thinking or fast and accurate reactions?

Parental Assessment:

Never underestimate how well you know your own child. How do you think they are performing? Is your child a quick learner? Do they enjoy academic study? Are they quick and accurate in their learning?

No one piece of information can determine your child's ability, but a combination can give you a good indication of how your child might perform in the 11+ examination. We can now look at each of these in more detail to help you make an accurate assessment.

Bond Placement Tests

The importance of the Bond Placement Tests is to highlight the level your child is at in the four 11+ subjects, with an additional spelling age and vocabulary test, to help you assess your child. This can be considered in terms of the time left to study and the level your child has achieved. Following the step-by-step plans will help make the most of the time available and will suggest the best course of action for your child to follow in order to give them the best preparation for the 11+ exam.

> ### ✓ HINT
>
> *Remember that your school of choice might only pick one or two of the test areas for their 11+ exam, so bear this in mind.*

SATs / CATs / PIEs / PIMs Results

These results show how well your child is performing compared to a national average. The 11+ exam is to determine the top performing pupils to select for grammar and independent school entry. A child who is average or below average in their SATs results is less likely to perform well in their 11+ exam. By the end of Year 6 the SATs national average is for your child to have reached Level 4b in maths and English. The CATs is a cognitive assessment that tests verbal reasoning, non-verbal reasoning, maths and vocabulary and provides a standardised score that shows how your child has performed against a national average. The Progress in English (PIEs) and Progress in Maths (PIMs) are set by some schools and again, these provide a standardised score so that you know how your child has performed against a national average. The CATs, PIEs and PIMs can provide a more specific score than the SATs so it can be easier to tell exactly how close your child is to the national average for their age, but it is only the SATs that are required in state schools so do not be surprised if your primary school only uses the SATs.

School Report

Your child's teacher and the school report can offer an insight into how your child is likely to perform. Is your child above average in maths and English? Does your child's school have a good academic reputation? How does the school year compare in terms of ability? You might have a child who is doing reasonably well, but against the national average they would be top and will be more than capable of passing the 11+. Sadly the opposite is also true and your child might be top in their school, but compared to the national average, they may be average or even lower than average. Teachers are qualified and experienced specialists who see many pupils over the years so that they can provide reliable feedback for most children and this information is so important. Although it is rare, there are occasions when a child is not accurately assessed for a variety of reasons.

From my own experience I remember one pupil in particular who had gone through his primary school in the bottom set, was pulled out of lessons for extra help in both numeracy and literacy, but was still not coping at all with even the basics. He came to me for additional help to ensure he stayed in mainstream education, but it appeared clear that this boy was extremely academic. I assessed him and found him to be well above the national average and understandably, his parents laughed and could not accept my findings. They were, however, open enough to give me the opportunity to work with the boy and he excelled. I worked with him for ten months for an hour a week. When the parents asked the school to put him in for the 11+ exam, the school strongly suggested that he would not understand the paper let alone stand any chance of passing it. He scored 97%, went straight into grammar school, remained in the top set and walked out with As and A*s in his GCSEs and is expected to gain the same in his A levels.

I would stress that this is unusual and most class teachers get the right assessment of their pupils and when they do not, it can be down to a number of 'fixable' reasons. Sometimes a child has been absent when tests were administered, sometimes a child is unable to see the board properly or unable to hear properly. Sometimes a child just does not perform well in a large classroom either by withdrawing or showing disruptive behaviour and this can also obscure their academic potential.

Parental Assessment

Don't forget that you know your child and their capabilities. Do you really feel they are able to pass the 11+ and do all the indications point to a child who is above average and likely to do well? Just as important is the rest of your child's education. Do you feel confident that they will thrive in a grammar school or will they be lucky to just survive? If you don't choose a selective education, does your child have the nature to reach their full potential anyway or are they likely to drift? Is your child happy to do homework or are you already having to nag them? Where will your child get the best education for them? Will the school cater for your child's interests in sports, music, technology, languages, religion or arts etc. and is this important?

Reading and Spelling Age

One question to ask the school or to check on the school report is your child's reading and spelling age if they provide it. Children who have a high spelling and reading age are likely to find the English and verbal reasoning tests easier than children who struggle with reading and spellings. Fluent reading and understanding is important in a timed test so your child will ideally have an above average reading age, although I have personally found that a score of at least two years ahead does make a significant difference in the English and verbal reasoning exams.

Children who do well with their spelling tests each week are not as well-prepared as children who consolidate their spellings and have many spellings in their long-term memory. A quick way of checking this is to complete a 50 word spelling test with your child asking them for words that were given five or six months previously. Mark their results and double the score to give you a percentage. If you child is scoring 85% +, you have a child with strong spelling skills. If however your child scored well five or six months ago, but has scored poorly now, you know that they may have excellent short-term memory skills, not spelling skills.

✅ TOP TIP!

Check the Bond How To Do 11+ English for advice and suggested book lists to help with your child's reading (see Appendix B for details) and try giving your child regular consolidation spelling tests to make sure their spellings are secure.

Logic Games

Does your child enjoy problem solving, crosswords, puzzles, riddles and logic games? Are they good at jigsaws, sliding puzzles and mathematical games? All of these are a good indication of a child's ability to grasp ideas of logic and problem solving and are invaluable in the verbal reasoning and non-verbal reasoning tests.

✅ HINT

There are lots of puzzle books available at newsagents and a huge range of apps for mobiles and tablets that can add fun and variety to skill building.

General Knowledge

This is one key area that can really help a child in comprehension, verbal reasoning and building vocabulary. It is fantastic to take children to museums, galleries and exhibitions to provide them with the benefits of travel and cultural exchange, but you might not have considered the more inexpensive ways of building knowledge all of the time. Here is my top ten:

1) Encourage your child to food shop with you and point out the wide range of foods available by type. (Dairy, pulses, root vegetables, cereals etc.)

2) Buy a selection of fruit and vegetables, especially the more unusual, to try.

3) Does your local park or nature reserve have a bird hide with information on local birds?

4) Take a walk around a garden centre to look specifically at trees or shrubs or flowers.

5) Baking even the most basic biscuits and cakes or cooking the main meal and converting the recipe to make more or less, gives your child the opportunity to measure, weigh, convert and to follow instructions in addition to using useful terms and utensils.

6) Walk around a village, town or city to look at the types of shops and buildings available.

7) Encourage your child to 'interview' family members to find out about what jobs people do, or used to do, what hobbies they have or where they have travelled.

8) Visit a working farm to look at the animals and to find the right names for the male, female, baby animal and the name of the animal homes or to find out what crops are grown and which are cereal and which are fruit and vegetable.

9) Look at colour samples to extend knowledge (for example, rose, cerise, salmon and coral are all pink. Olive, sage, mint and khaki are all green).

10) Look at the many art galleries that show their works online or borrow a library book on artists, musicians, instruments of the orchestra etc.

Build Up a Picture of Your Child's Ability

The more we can think of educating the whole child in a holistic way, the more we create and strengthen the skills that underpin many of the 11+ tests. Focusing all of your energy to push a child through an exam has limited benefits when you could open up an exciting world of education and learning for your child. The more rounded and rich their learning experience is, the more advantage your child will have and this can begin from the moment of birth. It is never too soon and never too late. It is surprising how many extremely bright children can struggle with a verbal reasoning exam because they lack general knowledge and vocabulary. It is also surprising how well a 'just above average' child can do if they have a wider range of vocabulary and knowledge.

Realistic Expectations

Passing the 11+ isn't about fluking it or being lucky on the day. It is a sifting system to separate children by their academic ability. Tutoring your child is useful in giving them self-confidence and strengthening their weak areas, but it is important to be realistic. If your child is clearly not capable of the 11+ without an awful lot of extra help, you may be able to push them to a certain extent, but how much time do you have and will they ever reach the standard required? It's also important to remember that passing the 11+ is only the start of it. If they should scrape through, how will they cope in an academic school that will push their pupils on a constant basis? Could you and your child cope with this on a daily basis for the next five, six or seven years? That is a lot of pressure for a teenager to be under and they may end up gaining far fewer or lower graded academic qualifications than the child who works at their own natural pace and succeeds in a less pressured school environment. Every parent wants the best for their child, but what is best for your child may not necessarily be the 11+ and a grammar school education.

Bond Placement Tests

 Why are the Bond Placement Tests useful?

The Bond Placement Tests included in this book are a vital stage in assessing your child. The results of these tests can help you decide at what level your child is and what books they need to progress towards the 11+ exam. They can help to highlight areas of strength and weakness so that a study plan can be put into place.

 When should my child sit the Bond Placement Tests?

Although these tests can be used at any time, the best time would be between 18 and 12 months before the 11+ exam takes place. This leaves you with optimum time for preparing your child, but however long you have before the exam, it is worth completing these tests.

 What if my child is sitting both the grammar school and private school exams?

The Bond Placement Tests are suitable for all children whether you are considering a grammar school or private school. You will need to check what subjects your schools use in the 11+ exam and then use the corresponding tests provided here.

Does my child need to sit all four tests?

The Bond Placement Tests are suitable for wherever you live as different LEAs use different tests. You will need to check what subjects your LEA or individual school is using and then use the corresponding tests provided here. Remember that English and maths underpin the verbal reasoning 11+ exams, so a good overall knowledge of these subjects will be needed even if your LEA just uses the verbal reasoning paper. The spelling age and vocabulary tests are suitable for both the English and verbal reasoning exams.

 What is the difference between multiple choice and standard format exams?

Some 11+ exams are in standard format, meaning that children will write their answers beside the questions on their 11+ exam paper. The multiple-choice paper has a separate answer booklet and children mark their answers out of a choice of options. The questions are not necessarily different, just the marking system. The tests here are in standard format, but are to be used by all children regardless of what your area does. It is recommended that all children follow a standard format system of learning until they are ready for test papers and at that level, you can then introduce the multiple choice paper. This is

Bond Placement
TESTS

- Verbal Reasoning
- English
- Maths
- Non-verbal Reasoning
- Vocabulary

VERBAL REASONING

LEVEL 1

The alphabet is here to help you with the first two questions:

A B C D E F G H I J K L M N O P Q R S T U V W X Y Z

Fill in the gaps in the following sequences:

Example: Z1 is to Y2 as X3 is to _____   Answer: W4

1 A35 is to B40 as C45 is to _____   **2** 29A is to 31B as 33C is to _____ | 2 |

Fill in the missing numbers in each sequence:

Example: 100   90   80   70   60   _____   40   Answer: 50

3 1   2   4   7   _____   16   **4** 40   36   _____   28   24   20 _____ | 2 |

Complete these sums:

Example: 7 x 6 = 50 – _____   Answer: 8 (42 = 50 – 8)

5 4 + 6 + 8 = 3 × _____   **6** 44 ÷ 11 = 2 × _____ | 2 |

Underline one word in the bracket to make each expression correct:

Example: Dog is to puppy as cat is to (paws, <u>kitten</u>, fluffy)

7 Boy is to girl as man is to (adult, person, woman) | 1 |

8 Mountain is to high as valley is to (fast, low, slow) | 1 |

Underline the two words that are made from the same letters:

Example: nest   <u>stun</u>   stem   <u>nuts</u>   meet

9 mate   meet   term   atom   team | 1 |

10 site   stem   mast   seat   teas | 1 |

| **10** |
| TOTAL LEVEL 1 |

LEVEL 2

Complete the following sentences by selecting one word from each group of words given in the brackets. Underline the words selected:

Example: The orange leaves of (spring, winter, <u>autumn</u>) were (<u>falling</u>, green, open) on the floor.

1 The old man (smiled, yawned, laughed) because he was (tired, worried, ill) and wanted to go to (hospital, bed, shops). | 1 |

2 She turned on the (lights, curtain, towels) as it was getting (light, dark, sunny). | 1 |

Underline the pair of words most similar in meaning:

Example: hot, cold   wet, dry   <u>easy, simple</u>

3 young, old   brief, short   good, bad   **4** talk, speak   read, story   bed, time | 2 |

Underline the two words, one from each group, that go together to form a new word. The word in the first group always comes first.

Example: (<u>so</u>, to, no) (down, <u>up</u>, over)

5 (birth, help, cradle) (less, more, much)   **6** (let, come, in) (room, doors, stairs) | 2 |

Find the three-letter word that can be added to the letters in capitals, to make a new word that will make sense. Write the word in the space.

Example: The footballer SCO a goal.   Answer: RED (The footballer scored a goal)

7 When the curtains were DN the light flooded in. _____ | 1 |

8 We FOLED the path to the sea. _____ | 1 |

Find a letter that will end the first word and begin the second.

Example: MAL _____ NEMY   Answer: E (MALE and ENEMY)

9 MOS _____ IME   **10** RIC _____ OME | 2 |

| **10** |
| TOTAL LEVEL 2 |

LEVEL 3

Underline the word that has the same meaning as the word in capital letters.

Example: TIRED slow <u>weary</u> fast lively silly

1 ABBREVIATE   disown   repeat   lengthen   shorten   delay | 1 |

2 PURSUE   run   follow   quarrel   fight   hurt | 1 |

3 PARDON   slave   forgive   rude   imprison   hate | 1 |

Find a word that can be put in front of each of the following words to make new compound words.

Example: day set burn shine   Answer: SUN (Sunday, sunset, sunburn, sunshine)

4 cream   hockey   skating   berg   _____ | 1 |

5 root   load   stairs   turn   _____ | 1 |

6 house   finch   fingers   grocer   _____ | 1 |

Underline the two words that need to change place for the sentence to make sense.

Example: The <u>trees</u> were resting beneath the <u>elephants</u>.

7 I down the flowerpot put.

8 It is wilting and the flowers are hot. | 2

9 We must turn until it is our wait. | 1

Underline the word that cannot be made from the letters of the word in capitals.

Example: ELEPHANT   ant   <u>bee</u>   pan   let   pea

10 FORGIVEN   grief   given   grove   green   give | 1

11 SERVICING   vices   singe   serve   giver   grins | 1

12 SUNSHINE   shine   shins   shuns   sheen   sushi | 1

Give the next number in the following sequences:

Example: 9972   9881   9790   9609   _____   Answer: 9518

13 1   20   2   19   _____

14 319   428   537   646   _____ | 2

15 1   8   27   64   _____ | 1

15

LEVEL 4

Underline two words, one from each group, which are opposite in meaning.

Example: (<u>reduce</u>, sale, market) (bargain, <u>increase</u>, shopping)

1 (annoy, discomfort, reward) (punishment, painless, distress) | 1

2 (slave, expensive, free) (work, dear, enslave) | 1

3 (cause, perfect, amazed) (error, flawed, flat) | 1

Write these words in alphabetical order:

Example: nat, ant, tan, tin, nit   Answer: ant, nat, nit, tan, tin

4 precise   precious   pretty   present   prettier

_____ | 1

5 graphic   graph   gracious   graphite   graceful

_____ | 1

Write the four-letter word hidden at the end of one word and the beginning of the next word. The order of the letters must not be changed.

Example: He liked fish and chips = hand

6   The house was surrounded by a circular drive.   _____ | 1 |

7   They have rye bread for breakfast.   _____ | 1 |

8   So dad rescued the kitten from the tree.   _____ | 1 |

The alphabet is here to help you with the next two questions:

A B C D E F G H I J K L M N O P Q R S T U V W X Y Z

The word HOLDER is written in code as IPMEFS. Encode these words using the same code.

9   LOSE = _____   10   HOLE = _____ | 2 |

If A = 1, B = 3, C = 5, D = 6, E = 10 and F = 12, what is the value of the following words if the letters are added together:

Example: CAFÉ = 5 + 1 + 12 + 10 = 28

11   FACE = _____   12   FADED = _____ | 2 |

> Grace, Juliet, Megan, Lucy and Laura are all learning to dance. Grace loves Jazz and Ballet. Juliet hates Ballet but loves everything else. Megan loves Classical, Tap and Ballet. Lucy doesn't like Jazz, Classical and Folk. Laura likes Tap best, but she also likes Folk.

13   Which is the most popular dance?   _____ | 1 |

14   Who likes the most dances?   _____ | 1 |

15   Who likes Classical dance?   _____ | 1 |

15
TOTAL
LEVEL 4

Verbal Reasoning Scores:				
	LEVEL 1	LEVEL 2	LEVEL 3	LEVEL 4
SCORE:				

ENGLISH

LEVEL 1

Circle the pronouns in each sentence.   *Example:* (We) *went to the caravan.*

1 I love cheese on toast.

2 Where has she gone?

`2`

With a line, match each word with its definition.

3 Foul   a baby horse
   Daffodil   a cold-blooded animal
   Foal   to break the rules
   Reptile   a spring flower

`1`

4 Several   someone who serves
   Nostril   more than a few but not all
   Server   clouds of gas and small bits of solid material
   Smoke   the opening at the end of your nose

`1`

Underline the root in each word.   *Example: Un*happy

5 Unclear

6 Impatiently

`2`

Underline the correct word in brackets to make sense of each sentence.

*Example: The dog (*ate* / eated) his breakfast.*

7 The sea (was / were) peaceful and calm.

8 The baby (drank / drinked) the milk.

`2`

Change these words into the past tense.   *Example: See* _____   *Answer: Saw*

9 Help _____

10 Do _____

`2`

`10`
TOTAL LEVEL 1

LEVEL 2

Put these words in the present tense:

Example: thought _____   *Answer: think*

1 Drank _____

2 Crept _____

`2`

Add the missing apostrophe to these nouns:

Example: Three cats' home

3 Daniels rabbit

4 The milkmans overalls

`2`

Write the letter that matches the expression with its meaning.

5 a) a wet blanket   1) filled with energy and high spirits

    b) full of beans   2) a keen reader

    c) bookworm   3) a miserable person

                                                   `1`

6 a) pins and needles   1) great success

    b) horse play   2) tingling cramp

    c) with flying colours   3) rough and boisterous   `1`

Write two examples of each word group used in the following passage:

> The two little birds sat stiffly on the thin branch. They patiently waited for their busy father to feed them.

7	Adjective		
8	Adverb		
9	Noun		
10	Verb		

`1`
`1`
`1`
`1`

10
TOTAL
LEVEL 2

LEVEL 3

Read this poem and then answer the following questions:

> *Autumn Time*
>
> Golden yellow butter pouring through the window,
> White, fluffy sheep, scampering through the sky,
> The brightest paint box blue, what a lovely backdrop,
> That's what I see with my artist's eye.
>
> Green, frothy bubbles bend and squash under my feet,
> Gifts from the trees, crunchy, crisp and dry.
> Trees left with bony arms that wave goodbye to me.
> That's what I see with my artist's eye.

1 How does the poet refer to the clouds?

    a) Golden yellow butter   c) The brightest paint box blue

    b) White, fluffy sheep   d) A lovely backdrop   `1`

2 What do you think the 'golden yellow butter' is?

    a) The summer sky   b) Yellow-tipped clouds

    c) The sun's rays   d) Butter-coloured paint

1

3 What phrase describes the grass?

    a) White, fluffy sheep   b) Green, frothy bubbles

    c) Gifts from the trees   d) Crunchy, crisp and dry

1

4 What are the 'gifts from the trees'?

    a) Fruit   b) Nuts

    c) Leaves   d) Branches

1

5 Why has the tree got waving, bony arms?

    a) The branches are thin because the trees is slender.

    b) The branches are bare because it is autumn time.

    c) The trees are friendly so the branches are waving.

    d) The trees are angry with spiky branches.

1

Add a connective word to join these clauses together:

Example: Chrissy needs help from Nicky ___because___ she cannot button up her coat.

6 I need that book _____ it is too high for me to reach.

1

7 Jon is my best friend _____ we play board games together.

1

8 The children were noisy _____ the teacher walked in.

1

Make three compound words using these words:

Example: me, tend, at, so = meat, some, attend

9 out   under   standing   with   let   line

1

Underline the correctly spelt words.

Example: Philip had (red / <u>read</u>) his book with (<u>interest</u> / intrest).

10 The fish were (silvery / silvary) and (slipery / slippery).

1

11 The (libary / library) was well (equipt / equipped).

1

12 He (might / mite) buy a (magazine / magasine).

1

13 She (tried / tired) to (seperate / separate) them.

1

Add both a prefix and a suffix to each word to make one new word.

Example: happy   *Answer: unhappiness*

14 Mind _____   **15** Equal _____ | 2 |

| 15 |
TOTAL
LEVEL 3

LEVEL 4

Write a short definition for each of these words:

1 Lubricate _____ | 1 |

2 Abbreviate _____ | 1 |

3 Resolve _____ | 1 |

Find the five words that are spelt incorrectly in this passage and write them out with the correct spelling:

> The casle was old and bleak. It had a moat running around it but the stagnant water was filthy and green. She bit her tong as she looked at the half derelict building and wanderd what had purswaded her farher to buy it.

4 _____   **5** _____   **6** _____ | 3 |

7 _____   **8** _____ | 2 |

Read this passage:

> I am good at maths, but I struggle with English. I have never read a book, let alone seen a play, although we did one scene of *Macbeth* last term. Best of all, I like PE because I get to play football every Wednesday. My team kit is red and white so I always look smart. My worst subject is science because I cannot understand it. There are too many things to remember and my class are not that good.

Complete the table using words from the text above:

9	Proper nouns				1
10	Collective nouns				1
11	Pairs of antonyms				1
12	Pairs of homophones				1

Write six synonyms for the word 'walk'.

13 _____

Underline the sentences that are written in reported speech:

14 "Are you ready yet?" asked Tom.   Tom had asked if he was ready.

    Tom asked, "Are you ready yet?"   Tom asked him if he was ready

Rewrite this text with the correct punctuation and capital letters added:

> the sun beamed down so we packed a picnic of sandwiches pie salad fruit and
> thick slices of cake then off we drove for a day out following the pretty roads
> we set off for llanidloes in wales we unpacked the car and settled ourselves
> beside the lake

15-20 _____

_____

_____

_____

_____

_____

_____

English Scores:				
	LEVEL 1	LEVEL 2	LEVEL 3	LEVEL 4
SCORE:				

MATHS

A chef places four rows of pasties in the oven. There are six pasties on each of the four rows.

1 How many pasties does the chef bake? _____ `1`

2 Write the number 'one thousand and seven' in figures. _____ `1`

Put a < or a > sign in each of the following spaces:

3 $(7 + 2)$ _____ 8 $(2 + 6)$ _____ 7 `1`

4 $(5 + 4)$ _____ 10 $(3 + 5)$ _____ 6 `1`

What are the answers to these equations?

5 $13 + 27 =$ _____ $43 + 36 =$ _____ `1`

6 $82 - 63 =$ _____ $96 - 33 =$ _____ `1`

Underline the correct answer:

7 $56 \div 8 = (6, 7, 8, 9)$ **8** $7 \times 7 = (42, 48, 49, 56)$ `2`

9 $81 - 9 = (72, 73, 74, 77)$ **10** $4 \times 12 = (36, 45, 48, 50)$ `2`

`10`
TOTAL LEVEL 1

LEVEL 2

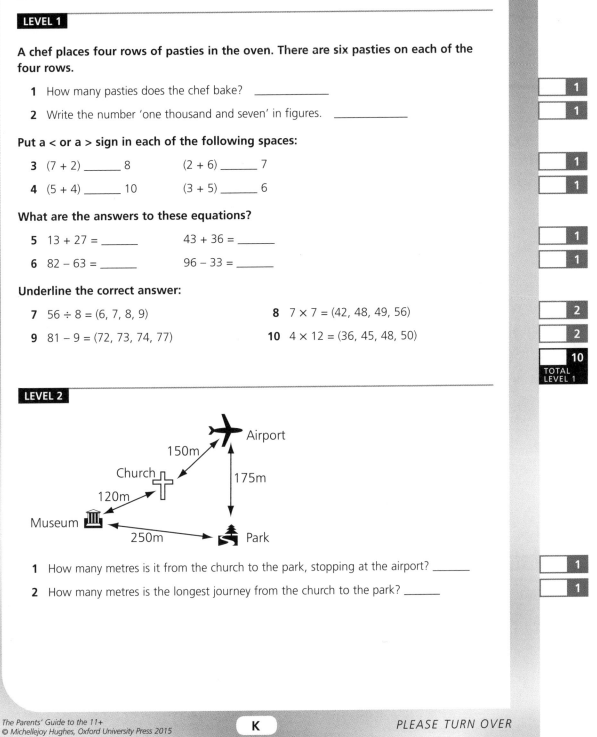

1 How many metres is it from the church to the park, stopping at the airport? _____ `1`

2 How many metres is the longest journey from the church to the park? _____ `1`

Fill in the gaps in the multiplication table:

3	×			4
4		10	15	
5	10			
6			45	

1
1
1
1

Name these shapes:

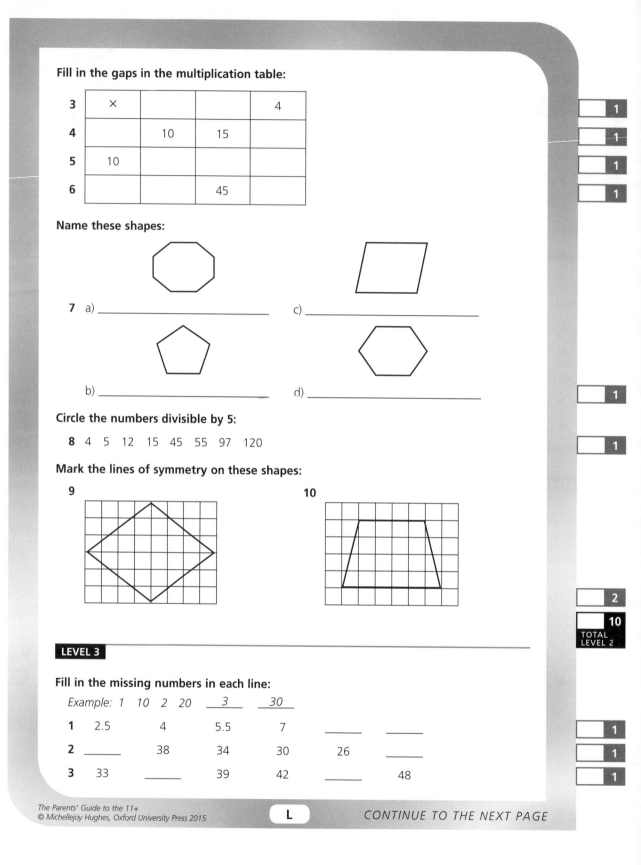

7 a) _____

c) _____

b) _____

d) _____

1

Circle the numbers divisible by 5:

8   4   5   12   15   45   55   97   120

1

Mark the lines of symmetry on these shapes:

9

10

2

10

TOTAL
LEVEL 2

LEVEL 3

Fill in the missing numbers in each line:

Example: 1   10   2   20   __3__   __30__

1   2.5   4   5.5   7   _____   _____

1

2   _____   38   34   30   26   _____

1

3   33   _____   39   42   _____   48

1
1

What are the answers to these equations?

Example: 329 × 10 = 3290

4 468 × 7 = _____

5 452 × 4 = _____

6 372 × 8 = _____

7 987 × 9 = _____

`2`

`2`

Underline the correct answer:

8 10 × 1000 =   100000   10000   101000   1010

9 10 ÷ 100 =   0.1   0.01   0.001   1

10 0.472 × 10 =   4.72   47.2   0.0472   472

`1`

`1`

`1`

I need to wrap these tins of biscuits up and each tin shows how much wrapping paper I need. Now answer the following questions by filling in the spaces correctly:

A   B   C   D   E

63 cm²   21 cm²   18 cm²   16 cm²   14 cm²

11 Tin _____ requires three times the amount of paper as tin _____.

12 Tin _____ requires half as much paper again as tin _____.

13 If I wrapped up tins C, D and E I would need _____ paper.

`1`

`1`

`1`

There are 297 children in Year 6. For every 14 girls there are 13 boys:

14 There are _____ boys and _____ girls in Year 6.

`1`

There are 50 teachers in the school. For every two male teachers there are three female teachers.

15 There are _____ male teachers and _____ female teachers.

`1`

`15`

TOTAL LEVEL 3

Underline the correct answer in each line:

Example: $42.3 + 17.9 =$ <u>*60.2*</u>   *602*   *6.02*   *60.12*

1 $10 - 1.99 =$ 9.11   8.01   11.9   9.01

2 $2.7 \times 200 =$ 5.4   540   54.0   0.54

3 $\frac{1}{2} \div \frac{3}{4} =$ $\frac{1}{3}$ $\frac{1}{4}$ $\frac{2}{3}$ $\frac{3}{8}$

Look at the following shapes and then complete table A:

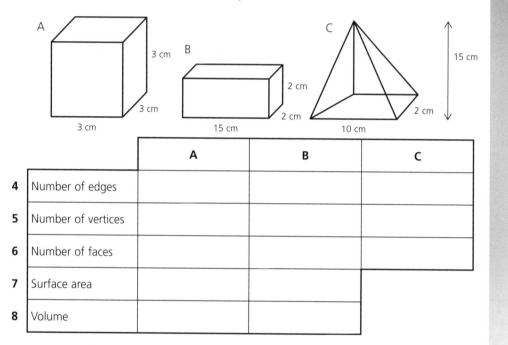

	A	**B**	**C**
4 Number of edges			
5 Number of vertices			
6 Number of faces			
7 Surface area			
8 Volume			

Complete the following cost and profit table:

9 Wholesale price	£18.75		£5.13	£196.50		93p
10 Retail price	£23.50	£70.20		£235.25	£13.50	£1.12
11 Profit		£11.35	97p		£2.19	19p

Write these decimals as fractions:

Example: $4.5 = 4\frac{1}{2}$

12 $3.125 =$ _____

13 $4.05 =$ _____

14) $7.62 =$ _____

15) $9.07 =$ _____

	2
	2
	15

TOTAL
LEVEL 4

Maths Scores:				
	LEVEL 1	LEVEL 2	LEVEL 3	LEVEL 4
SCORE:				

NON-VERBAL REASONING

LEVEL 1

Put a circle round the odd one out on both lines:

1

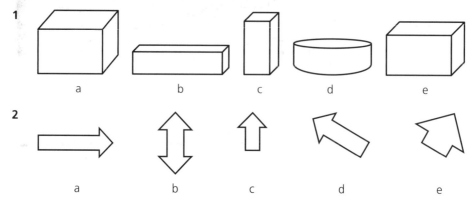

a   b   c   d   e

2

a   b   c   d   e

Circle the correct picture on the right, which is a reflection of the picture on the left of the dotted mirror line.

3

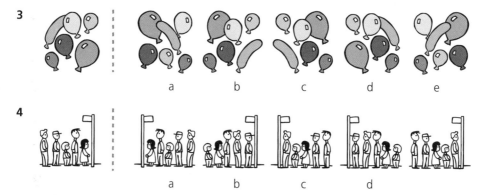

a   b   c   d   e

4

a   b   c   d

Draw the rest of these shapes as they would be if reflected in the mirror.

5   **6**

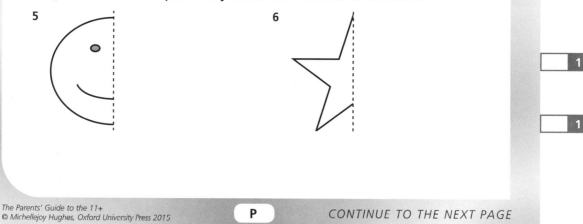

1   1   1   1   1   1

Circle the odd shape out:

7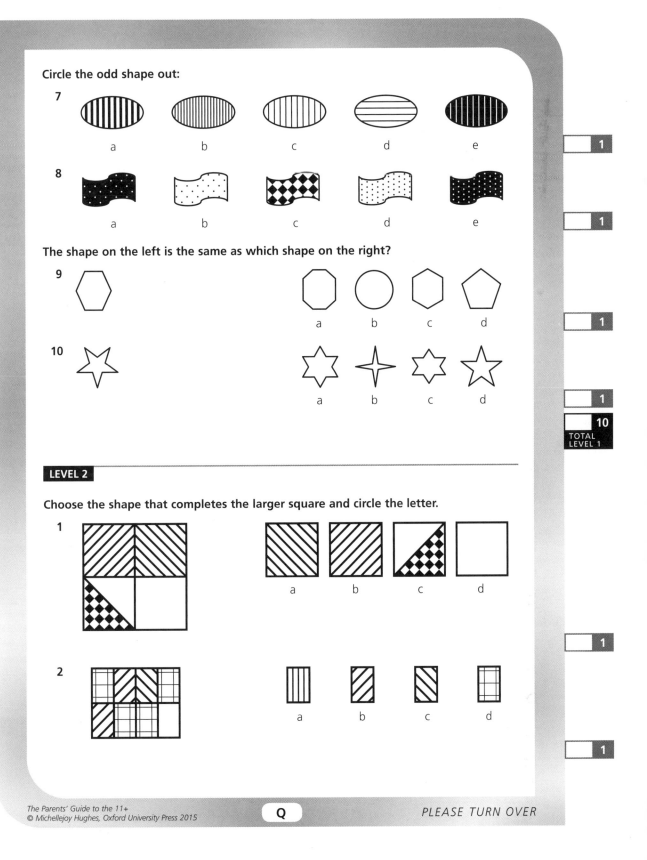

    a   b   c   d   e

8

    a   b   c   d   e

The shape on the left is the same as which shape on the right?

9

    a   b   c   d

10

    a   b   c   d

TOTAL LEVEL 1 10

LEVEL 2

Choose the shape that completes the larger square and circle the letter.

1

    a   b   c   d

2

    a   b   c   d

Which picture comes next? Circle the letter.

3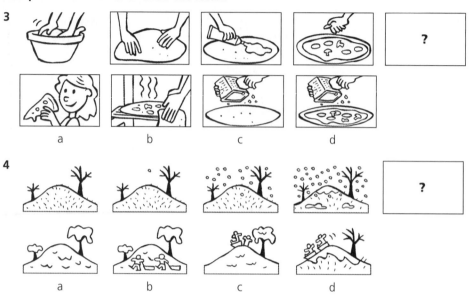

a   b   c   d

4

a   b   c   d

Match the nets with their cubes by joining them together with a line:

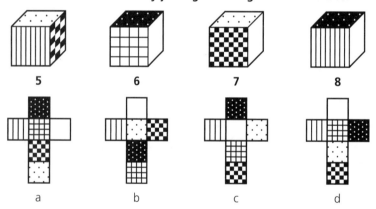

5   6   7   8

a   b   c   d

Circle the one shape on the right that does not fit with the shape on the left:

9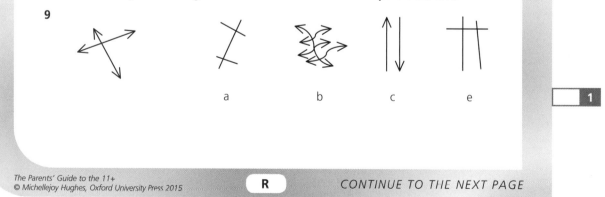

a   b   c   e

| 1 |
| 1 |
| 4 |
| 1 |

10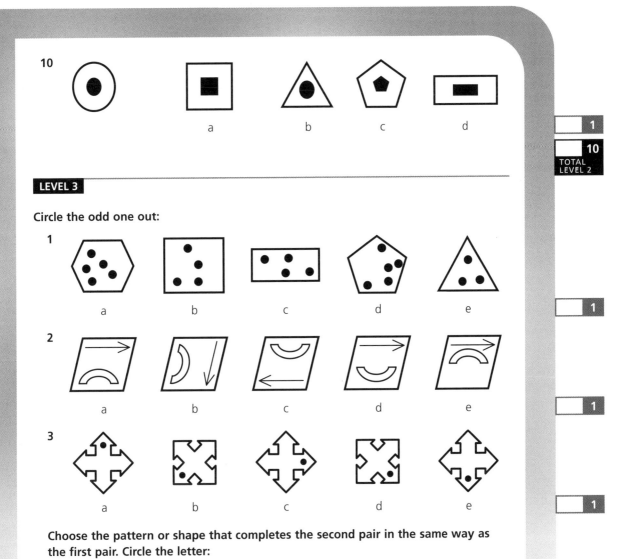

a   b   c   d

1

10
TOTAL
LEVEL 2

LEVEL 3

Circle the odd one out:

1

a   b   c   d   e

2

a   b   c   d   e

3

a   b   c   d   e

Choose the pattern or shape that completes the second pair in the same way as the first pair. Circle the letter:

4   is to   as   is to

a   b   c   d

5   is to   as   is to

a   b   c   d

1

1

1

1

1

In which larger shape or pattern is the smaller shape hidden? Circle the letter:

6

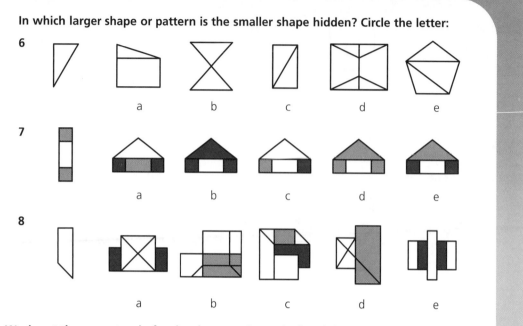

a   b   c   d   e

7

a   b   c   d   e

8

a   b   c   d   e

Work out the correct code for the shape at the end of each line. Write the answer on the line:

9

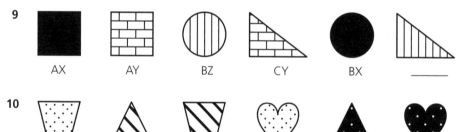

AX   AY   BZ   CY   BX   _____

10

S1   T2   S2   U1   T3   _____

Which shape or pattern completes the bigger pattern? Circle the letter.

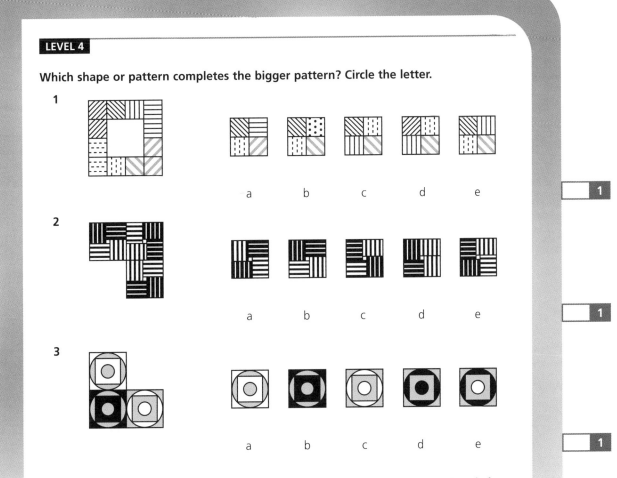

1

a b c d e

2

a b c d e

3

a b c d e

Compare the two shapes on the left. Which other shape goes with this pair? Circle the letter.

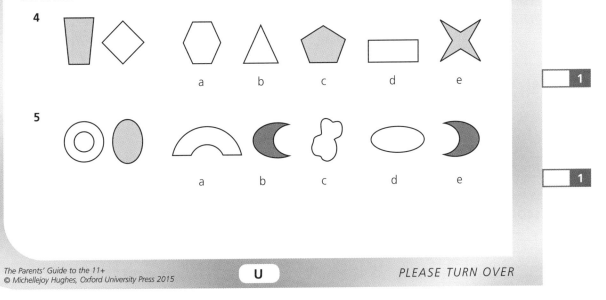

4

a b c d e

5

a b c d e

Which is the odd one out? Circle the letter.

6

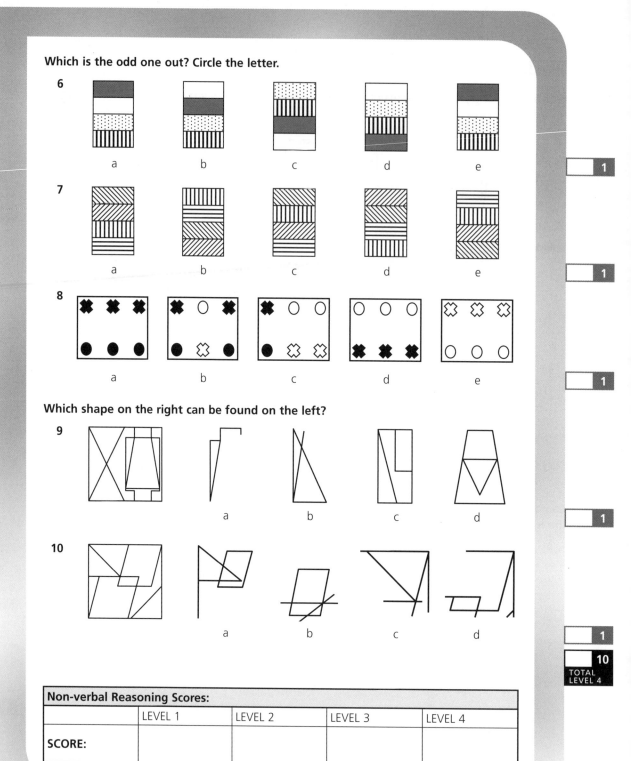

a   b   c   d   e

7

a   b   c   d   e

8

a   b   c   d   e

Which shape on the right can be found on the left?

9

a   b   c   d

10

a   b   c   d

1

1

1

1

1

10

TOTAL
LEVEL 4

Non-verbal Reasoning Scores:				
	LEVEL 1	LEVEL 2	LEVEL 3	LEVEL 4
SCORE:				

VOCABULARY / GENERAL KNOWLEDGE TEST

Read out the following questions to your child and make a tally chart of the correct answers. However tempting, don't prompt your child or show any response to their answers as you won't get a genuine score. This test is timed with 60 seconds allowed for each question. Sometimes there are few questions needed within the minute and for other questions there are more questions in the same amount of time. This replicates some of the pressure of an actual exam while showing you how many words your child can recall under time pressure. The topics seem to swap and change which again replicates the more random nature of an exam.

1 Can you name six sports where we use a ball?

   Example: football, baseball, netball, golf, tennis, rugby, snooker, hockey

2 Can you name three countries that begin with the letter 'a'?

   Example: Australia, Austria, Albania, Afghanistan, Antigua, Andorra

3 Can you name three colours beginning with the letter 'b'?

   Example: brown, black, beige, burgundy, blue, bronze, buff

4 Can you name six rooms in a house?

   Example: kitchen, bedroom, living room, study, library, porch, hall, pantry

5 Can you name three root vegetables?

   Example: carrots, parsnips, turnips, potatoes, swede, yam, cassava

6 Can you name four trees?

   Example: oak, beech, birch, ash, hazel, pine, fir, yew, willow, rowan

7 Can you name four flowers?

   Example: rose, poppy, daisy, lily, viola, pansy, orchid, dahlia, buttercup

8 Can you name four metals?

   Example: copper, iron, zinc, gold, silver, lead, tin, aluminium, platinum

9 Can you name four items of food found in the dairy section of a shop?

   Example: milk, cream, yoghurt, cheese, crème fraiche, lassi, custard

10 Can you name four planets?

   Example: Mars, Venus, Mercury, Earth, Saturn, Jupiter, Neptune, Uranus

11 Can you name four gem stones?

   Example: ruby, sapphire, diamond, garnet, emerald, amethyst, topaz

12 Can you name six baby animal names?

   Example: foal, calf, cub, puppy, kitten, piglet, lamb, kid, kit, pup, leveret

13 Can you name six zoo animals?

Example: tiger, lion, giraffe, bat, snake, monkey, ape, wolf, bear, bison

14 Can you name five clothing materials?

Example: cotton, nylon, wool, silk, leather, polyester, acrylic, denim, lace

15 Can you name three types of hat?

Example: bonnet, fez, beret, beanie, fedora, bowler, kippah, kofia, cap

16 Can you name six farm animals?

Example: cow, horse, goat, sheep, pig, chickens, ducks, geese, donkey

17 Can you name four words beginning with the letter 'q'?

Example: quiz, quick, queue, quay, quiet, quite, quest, quilt, quack, quit

18 Can you name four garden birds?

Example: blackbird, wren, robin, thrush, finch, sparrow, blue tit, starling

19 Can you name four words beginning with the letter 'i'?

Example: in, inside, if, it, itself, individual, island, iron, impress, indigo

20 Can you name four buildings found in a town or city centre?

Example: theatre, cinema, town hall, library, museum, bank, office, shop

21 Can you name three types of boat?

Example: dinghy, canoe, kayak, trawler, yacht, liner, narrowboat, ferry

22 Can you name three fruits with stones in the middle of them?

Example: cherry, peach, apricot, damson, plum, greengage, avocado

23 Can you name three types of dance?

Example: ballet, jazz, ballroom, Latin, urban, street, tap, disco, popping

24 What does a tailor do?

Someone who makes clothes / sews clothes

25 What colours are olive, sage and khaki?

Green

26 What is an orchard?

A collection of fruit trees

27 If I have a dozen eggs, how many do I have?

Twelve

TOTAL SCORE: _____ %

because children need to understand how to do the questions first and then how to fill in the answer booklets as a final stage in their 11+ learning.

 Where can I buy the Bond Placement Tests?

The Bond Placement Tests are only available with this book. These tests have been created to form a solid structure on which to assess children. Each level corresponds with a Bond Assessment Papers workbook level, providing a seamless crossover from placement test to workbook progression. They work as an integrated part of the Bond system, which provides maximum support.

 Are the Bond Placement Tests just for the 11+?

Although they are perfect for the 11+ assessment, the maths and English tests are ideal for all children as they follow the National Curriculum guidelines that schools use and will ultimately help in preparation for school SATs exams.

 Does my child need to do all of the Bond Placement Tests in one go?

Allow your child 30 minutes of uninterrupted time to complete each test. There are four tests in total, which can be divided into four separate sessions of 30 minutes, or two sessions of 1 hour. The spelling and vocabulary test takes another 15 minutes each and can be taken in one sitting, or the spellings in one sitting and the vocabulary in another.

 Should I help my child or read through the paper with them?

It is really important that your child works through these tests without any help. Explain to your child that they are to do their best and not to worry about any questions they cannot complete, but to do as much as they can, making a guess at anything they are not sure of. Because the tests are timed, you might want to give them a 'half time' and a 'five minutes before the end' reminder. If your child has a specific learning difficulty where a scribe or reader would be provided in their exam, then please do take on the role of scribe and /or reader, but you should only do as much as an official would do without encouraging or leading your child.

 What is the spelling test for?

The spelling test is another useful assessment of your child's ability. Ideally your child will have a spelling age the same as or better than their actual age. The *Bond Spelling and Vocabulary* books (see Appendix B) are recommended if your child has a lower spelling age or wants to practise and develop their skills. The answers to the tests are at the back of this book (see Appendix C), so when your child has completed the tests, mark their answers, record their results in the results chart and then find out how to interpret them and create a Personal Learning Plan in Step 3.

 What is the vocabulary test for?

The vocabulary test is another useful assessment of your child's ability as it tests the general knowledge and breadth of vocabulary needed for the verbal reasoning and English tests. The answers to the tests are at the back of this book (see Appendix C), so when your child hascompleted the test, mark their answers, record their results in the results chart and then find out how to interpret them and create a Personal Learning Plan in Step 3.

Bond Placement Tests Checklist

My child will need to sit the following Bond Placement Tests:

☐ Maths   ☐ Non-verbal Reasoning

☐ English   ☐ Spelling Age Test

☐ Verbal Reasoning   ☐ Vocabulary Test

In order to do their best, your child will need the following:

● Pencil

● Eraser

● Pencil sharpener

● Flat surface to work on, e.g. table or desk

● A well-lit, quiet area to work

● Spare paper for any rough working

● A watch or clock to check timing

● The right time (You would be amazed how much the results can differ when the same child takes the test late at night in front of the television when they are hungry, thirsty, tired and grumpy!)

Find the Spelling Age

Another useful test for grading your child is a spelling test. It is worthwhile finding the spelling age of your child at the same time as taking the Bond Placement Tests and then every four months to check what progress has been made. The spelling test can be used for all primary school ages and is a useful guide as to how your child is progressing. The words selected here have been chosen to represent a cross-selection of graded high frequency words.

In order to find your child's spelling age, read out this list of 50 words for your child to write down. Repeat each word twice in a clear voice, but don't over pronounce the words. Allow your child a few seconds to write each word down, but if they are struggling, ask them to spell the word as they think it is. When the word is a homophone with an alternative spelling, or could be confused with another word, there are words given in the brackets that should be read out:

mat (The mat was on the floor.)	cut	rot	dad
bin (I threw the rubbish in the bin.)	pen	with	from
yard	good	dream	yearly
mind (Do you mind if I sit here?)	sooner	call	while
headache	mistake	height	large
island (We live on an island.)	bought	lamb	wealth
strayed	bargain	decrease	policy
style (I like that shoe style.)	valleys	library	museum
equally	cushion	similar	slippery
earlier	leisure	mortgage	generous
calves (The cow fed her calves.)	especially	immediate	separate
apparatus	equipped	politician	committee
permanent	difference		

When the test is over, compare the spellings with the words here. Allocate your child 1 mark for each correctly spelt word.

- Don't allow marks or half marks for 'almost right' words.
- Add up the total out of 50.
- Multiply the total by 2.
- Divide this number by 10.
- Add on 5.

Example 1:

Charlotte is 9 years and 8 months. Charlotte has a score of 27:

Multiply the total by 2	$27 \times 2 = 54$
Divide this by 10	$54 \div 10 = 5.4$
Add on 5	$5.4 + 5 = 10.4$

Charlotte's spelling age is 10 years and 4 months, which is higher than her real age by 8 months. As Charlotte's score is higher than her real age, it would indicate an advantage in English and verbal reasoning.

Example 2:

Leo is 10 years and 4 months. Leo has a score of 19:

Multiply the total by 2	$19 \times 2 = 38$
Divide this by 10	$38 \div 10 = 3.8$
Add on 5	$3.8 + 5 = 8.8$

Leo's spelling age is 8 years and 8 months, which is lower than his real age by 1 year and 8 months. As Leo's score is lower than average, it would indicate a disadvantage in English and verbal reasoning and Leo would need time to improve his spellings.

To help improve your child's spelling age, the *Bond Spelling and Vocabulary* books are recommended as they are designed to develop children's spelling and word knowledge. You can also find a spelling list of 100 words your child should know for the 11+ in the free resoures section of Bond's website: www.bond11plus.co.uk. *Bond How To Do 11+ English* develops word awareness and is ideal for 11+ pupils. (See Appendix B for details.)

Record the Results

When your child has completed the Bond Placement Tests, use the answer section in Appendix C to mark the papers. You then need to fill in the results chart (see page 67) to find where your child is at and what support they need. The results help you to work out the difference between your child's age and their spelling age, the percentage of their maths, English, verbal reasoning and non-verbal reasoning and the expected percentage based on the length of time left until the 11+ exam.

Here is an example of how to fill in and interpret the results:

Example 1: Kamran

Kamran sat the placement tests and here are his scores compared with his expected scores:

Age:	8 years 7 months			
Spelling Age:	10 years 9 months			
Spelling Age Difference:	**+ 2 years 2 months**			
Vocabulary	61%	Expected	67%	**Difference:** –6%
		MATHS	ENGLISH	VR	NON-VR
Level 1 (37–48 months to 11+)		10/10	10/10	9/10	6/10
Level 2 (25–36 months to 11+)		10/10	10/10	7/10	5/10
Level 3 (13–24 months to 11+)		8/15	10/15	2/15	4/10
Level 4 (0–12 months to 11+)		3/15	8/20	0/15	1/10
Total Score:		31/50	38/55	18/50	16/40
Total = % (100 ÷ 50 × 31) (100 ÷ 55 x 38) (100 ÷ 50 × 18) (100 ÷ 40 × 16)		62%	69%	36%	40%
Expected %		48%	48%	48%	48%
Difference:		**+14%**	**+21%**	**–12%**	**–8%**
Months To 11+ Exam: 24					

Example 2: Alice

Alice sat the placements tests and here are her scores compared with her expected scores:

Age:		9 years 11 months			
Spelling Age:		10 years 3 months			
Spelling Age Difference:		**+ 4 months**			
Vocabulary	67%	Expected	85%	**Difference:**	−18%
		MATHS	ENGLISH	VR	NON-VR
Level 1 (37–48 months to 11+)		10/10	10/10	9/10	10/10
Level 2 (25–36 months to 11+)		10/10	9/10	8/10	10/10
Level 3 (13–24 months to 11+)		12/15	6/15	0/15	4/10
Level 4 (0–12 months to 11+)		12/15	6/20	0/15	4/10
Total Score:		44/50	31/55	17/50	28/40
Total = % (100 ÷ 50 × 44) (100 ÷ 55 x 33) (100 ÷ 50 × 21) (100 ÷ 40 × 29 rounded to the nearest %)		88%	56%	34%	70%
Expected %		84%	84%	84%	84%
Difference:		**+4%**	**−28%**	**−50%**	**−14%**
Months To 11+ Exam: 6					

We can see that Kamran has a strong spelling age and is significantly stronger in his maths and English. We can see that in maths and English, Kamran has thorough knowledge in level 1 and 2 and is only struggling at level 3, which is to be expected as he has not yet covered all of the material in school. In terms of the verbal reasoning and non-verbal reasoning, these subjects are not taught in Kamran's school so this is the first time that he has seen these question types and has therefore scored extremely well. His vocabulary score is slightly below the expected scores and as Kamran has 24 months to prepare for the 11+ he is starting from a really strong position. He could choose to gradually work towards his 11+ or to begin in 18 months' time.

When we look at Alice's score, her percentages are higher than Kamran's, but her expected scores are much higher as she is older and has less time until the 11+ exam. If her 11+ exam was just maths, then Alice would have sufficient time to get used to the exam format and to revise any weak areas as her scores across all of the levels in maths is strong. If Alice has any other subject to cover, then she will have a lot of work to cover in a short space of time.

Here is the results chart for your child's results:

Age:					
Spelling Age:					
Spelling Age Difference:					
Vocabulary		Expected		**Difference:**	
		MATHS	ENGLISH	VR	NON-VR
Level 1 (37–48 months to 11+)					
Level 2 (25–36 months to 11+)					
Level 3 (13–24 months to 11+)					
Level 4 (0–12 months to 11+)					
Total Score:					
Total = % (100 ÷ 50 × ??) (100 ÷ 55 × ??) (100 ÷ 50 × ??) (100 ÷ 40 × ??) rounded to the nearest %)					
Expected %					
Difference:					
Months To 11+ Exam:					

Vocabulary Expected Scores by Months to 11+ Exam:											
Months	**48**	**47**	**46**	**45**	**44**	**43**	**42**	**41**	**40**	**39**	**38**	**37**
% score	43	44	45	46	47	48	49	50	51	52	53	54
Months	**36**	**35**	**34**	**33**	**32**	**31**	**30**	**29**	**28**	**27**	**26**	**25**
% score	55	56	57	58	59	60	61	62	63	64	65	66
Months	**24**	**23**	**22**	**21**	**20**	**19**	**18**	**17**	**16**	**15**	**14**	**13**
% score	67	68	69	70	71	72	73	74	75	76	77	78
Months	**12**	**11**	**10**	**9**	**8**	**7**	**6**	**5**	**4**	**3**	**2**	**1**
% score	79	80	81	82	83	84	85	86	87	88	89	90

Maths, English, VR and NVR Expected Scores by Month:											
Months	**48**	**47**	**46**	**45**	**44**	**43**	**42**	**41**	**40**	**39**	**38**	**37**
% score	0	2	4	6	8	10	12	14	16	18	20	22
Months	**36**	**35**	**34**	**33**	**32**	**31**	**30**	**29**	**28**	**27**	**26**	**25**
% score	24	26	28	30	32	34	36	38	40	42	44	46
Months	**24**	**23**	**22**	**21**	**20**	**19**	**18**	**17**	**16**	**15**	**14**	**13**
% score	48	50	52	54	56	58	60	62	64	66	68	70
Months	**12**	**11**	**10**	**9**	**8**	**7**	**6**	**5**	**4**	**3**	**2**	**1**
% score	72	74	76	78	80	82	84	86	88	90	92	94

In order to interpret your child's results, you need to confirm the relevant 11+ subjects for your area and then see what the results show in these subjects. If you have decided to put your child forward for the 11+ exam, you can now move on to Step 3 and learn how to create a personal action plan based on this results chart.

Checklist for Step 2 Success

☐ I know what the 11+ test consists of for the school(s) of my choice

☐ I've checked my child's current / predicted SATs scores

☐ I've checked my child's spelling age

☐ I've checked my child's reading age from their school

☐ I've consulted my child's school reports

☐ I've spoken with my child's school teacher

☐ I've set my child the Bond Placement Tests

☐ I've recorded the results of the Bond Placement Tests

☐ I've made a decision on my child sitting the 11+ exam

☐ I'm ready to move on to preparation for the exam

☐ I still need to find out more about:

....

....

....

....

....

....

....

....

STEP 3

Prepare for the Exam

- Know When To Start
- Develop Your Child's Learning Plan
- Apply Bond's Step-by-Step Action Plan
- Common Questions

- Motivate Your Child
- Minimise Stress for Everyone
- Deal With The Exam Day
- Checklist for Step 3 Success

◀ When is it a good time to start preparing for the 11⁺ test? ▶

◀ *My child is in Year 4 – is it too early to think about it yet? Should I be doing something now to get her ready?* ▶

◀ I know I've left it late as my child is sitting the 11⁺ in a few weeks. What can I do to help him? ▶

◀ *I don't know where to start and there are so many 11⁺ workbooks in the shops that I really have no idea where to begin. I don't want to waste any more time, but I need a quick, effective system.* ▶

◀ We have so much to do and so little time left, where do we start? ▶

◀ *How much does it cost to use the Bond 11⁺ system? Can I afford it?* ▶

Know When to Start

By now you will have assessed your child and will have decided whether you are going to enter your child for the 11⁺ exam. Ideally, you will have a clear 12 months from your preparation time to the actual date of the 11⁺ exam. If you have longer, congratulations, as you will have time to take it more gradually and apply less pressure on your child. If you have less than 12 months, you will need to decide how much you have to do with your child in the time between now and the exam. Try not to panic; even with a few days to go there is still plenty that you can do to help your child.

To make optimum use of the time you have available, you can devise a personal learning plan. This will show you which books you need to cover, and the amount of time your child has to work through them. Let's look back at Kamran and his results chart:

Age:	8 years 7 months			
Spelling Age:	10 years 9 months			
Spelling Age Difference:	**+ 2 years 2 months**			
Vocabulary:	61%	Expected:	67%	**Difference**:	**– 6%**
	MATHS	ENGLISH	VR	NON-VR
Level 1 (25–37 months to 11⁺)	31/33	29/33	20/33	20/33
Level 2 (13–24 months to 11⁺)	29/33	26/33	14/33	18/33
Level 3 (0–12 months to 11⁺)	2/33	15/33	3/33	4/33
Total = %	62%	70%	37%	42%
Expected %	48%	48%	48%	48%
Difference:	**+14%**	**+22%**	**–11%**	**–6%**
Months To 11⁺ Exam: 24				

We know that Kamran has strong spellings, maths and English and has only begun to struggle with material that he has not yet been taught in school. Kamran has no experience of verbal and non-verbal reasoning so he will need to work on these if he is tested in these subjects.

Kamran will actually be sitting the CEM 11⁺ exam. This means that he will need good strong skills across all four subjects using the CEM format. He also has 24 months before the exam, which is ideal. Kamran has expressed that because of a busy social life and a fair amount of school homework and extra-curricular clubs, he would prefer a small weekly amount of homework over a longer period of time. Kamran is an active reader and was keen not to lose this habit and with sports and music commitments, Kamran can devote 1 ½ hours a week to his 11+.

Using this information I devised the following learning plan for Kamran:

CEM EXAM STYLE:	CEM English/VR/Maths/NVR : Multiple Choice Format	
Month:	English/VR	Maths/NVR
September	Bond CEM English/VR 8–9 Bond English 10 Minute Tests 9–10	Bond CEM Maths/NVR 8–9 Bond Maths 10 Minute Tests 9–10
October	Bond CEM English/VR 8–9 Bond English 10 Minute Tests 9–10	Bond CEM Maths/NVR 8–9 Bond Maths 10 Minute Tests 9–10
November	Bond CEM English/VR 8–9 Bond English 10 Minute Tests 9–10	Bond CEM Maths/NVR 8–9 Bond Maths 10 Minute Tests 9–10
December	Bond Comprehension 9–10 Bond English 10 Minute Tests 9–10	Bond NVR 9–10 Book 1 Bond Maths 10 Minute Tests 9–10
January	Bond Comprehension 9–10 Bond English 10 Minute Tests 9–10	Bond NVR 9–10 Book 1 Bond Maths 10 Minute Tests 9–10
February	Bond Comprehension 9–10 Bond English 10 Minute Tests 9–10	Bond NVR 9–10 Book 2 Bond Maths 10 Minute Tests 9–10
March	Bond Comprehension 9–10 Bond English 10 Minute Tests 9–10	Bond NVR 9–10 Book 2 Bond Maths 10 Minute Tests 9–10
April	Bond CEM English/VR 9–10 Bond English 10 Minute Tests 10–11+	Bond CEM Maths/NVR 9–10 Bond Maths 10 Minute Tests 10–11+
May	Bond CEM English/VR 9–10 Bond English 10 Minute Tests 10–11+	Bond CEM Maths/NVR 9–10 Bond Maths 10 Minute Tests 10–11+
June	Bond CEM English/VR 9–10 Bond English 10 Minute Tests 10–11+	Bond CEM Maths/NVR 9–10 Bond Maths 10 Minute Tests 10–11+
July	Bond Comprehension 10–11+ Bond English 10 Minute Tests 10–11+	Bond NVR 10–11+ Book 1 Bond Maths 10 Minute Tests 10–11+
August	Bond Comprehension 10–11+ Bond English 10 Minute Tests 10–11+	Bond NVR 10–11+ Book 1 Bond Maths 10 Minute Tests 10–11+
September	Bond Comprehension 10–11+ Bond English 10 Minute Tests 10–11+	Bond NVR 10–11+ Book 2 Bond Maths 10 Minute Tests 10–11+
October	Bond Comprehension 10–11+ Bond English 10 Minute Tests 10–11+	Bond NVR 10–11+ Book 2 Bond Maths 10 Minute Tests 10–11+
November	Bond CEM English/VR 10–11+ Bond English 10 Minute Tests 11+–12+	Bond CEM Maths/NVR 10–11+ Bond Maths 10 Minute Tests 11–12+
December	Bond CEM English/VR 10–11+ Bond English 10 Minute Tests 11+–12+	Bond CEM Maths/NVR 10–11+ Bond Maths 10 Minute Tests 11–12+
January	Bond CEM English/VR 10–11+ Bond English 10 Minute Tests 11+–12+	Bond CEM Maths/NVR 10–11+ Bond Maths 10 Minute Tests 11–12+
February	Bond Comprehension 11+–12+ Bond English 10 Minute Tests 11+–12+	Bond NVR 11–12+ Book 1 Bond Maths 10 Minute Tests 11–12+
March	Bond Comprehension 11+–12+ Bond English 10 Minute Tests 11+–12+	Bond NVR 11–12+ Book 1 Bond Maths 10 Minute Tests 11–12+
April	Bond Comprehension 11+–12+ Bond English 10 Minute Tests 11+–12+	Bond NVR 11–12+ Book 2 Bond Maths 10 Minute Tests 11–12+
May	Bond Comprehension 11+–12+ Bond English 10 Minute Tests 11+–12+	Bond NVR 11–12+ Book 2 Bond Maths 10 Minute Tests 11–12+
June	Bond CEM Test Papers Set 1	
July	Bond CEM Test Papers Set 1/2	
August	Bond CEM Test Papers Set 2	

This learning plan would allow Kamran to cover the CEM exam style exam questions with the CEM books and test papers, but would also build up non-verbal reasoning and comprehension skills and consolidate English and maths skills with the '10 Minute Test' books. Spreading this work over 24 months would give Kamran an average of 1–1 ½ hours of 11+ study a week, giving him the opportunity to steadily build solid skills without a heavy commitment.

Let's look back at Alice and her results chart:

Age:	9 years 11 months			
Spelling Age:	10 years 3 months			
Spelling Age Difference:	**+ 4 months**			
Vocabulary	67%	Expected	85%	**Difference:**	**−18%**
		MATHS	ENGLISH	VR	NON-VR
Level 1 (37–48 months to 11+)		10/10	10/10	9/10	10/10
Level 2 (25–36 months to 11+)		10/10	9/10	8/10	10/10
Level 3 (13–24 months to 11+)		12/15	6/15	0/15	4/10
Level 4 (0–12 months to 11+)		12/15	6/20	0/15	4/10
Total Score:		44/50	31/55	17/50	28/40
Total = % (100 ÷ 50 × 44) (100 ÷ 55 x 33) (100 ÷ 50 × 21) (100 ÷ 40 × 29 rounded to the nearest %)		88%	56%	34%	70%
Expected %		84%	84%	84%	84%
Difference:		**+4%**	**−28%**	**−50%**	**−14%**
Months To 11+ Exam: 6					

It does make a huge difference to work in partnership with your child. Ask them how much 11+ work they feel that they can fit in each week and try to accommodate this. It will be much easier to motivate a child who has had input throughout the process. I've included a weekly timetable template in the appendix, that I use with those pupils who like to follow their learning plan at a daily level. Please do feel free to photocopy it or alter it if it helps your child.

Alice is highly motivated and is aware that she has a limited time before her 11+ exam. She understands that there is a lot to learn and as it is only for a short period of time, she is happy to do as much work as is necessary. She doesn't have many extra-curricular commitments and is happy to reduce her social life to push towards the 11+. Fortunately for her, the 11+ exam is a GL Assessment non-verbal reasoning test.

This is what I would suggest as a learning plan for Alice:

GL ASSESSMENT EXAM STYLE:	GL Non-Verbal Reasoning: Standard Format	
Month:	**Non-Verbal Reasoning**	
March	Bond NVR 9–10 Book 1	Bond NVR 9–10 Book 2
April	Bond NVR Stretch 9–10	Bond NVR 10 Minute Tests 9–10
May	Bond NVR 10–11+ Book 1	Bond NVR 10–11+ Book 2
June	Bond NVR Stretch 10–11+	Bond NVR 10 Minute Tests 10–11+
July	Bond NVR 11+–12 + Book 1	Bond NVR 11+–12+ Book 2
August	Bond NVR Standard Test Papers Set 1	Bond NVR Standard Test Papers Set 2

This would allow Alice to cover the GL Assessment non-verbal reasoning questions with the Bond books and test papers over a six month period. This would give Alice an average of 2½ hours of study a week providing her with solid non-verbal reasoning skills. If Alice had other subjects to study, or if she had a subject that she struggled with, she would find it difficult to fit in sufficient work, but this amount of work is achievable for her.

Develop Your Child's Learning Plan

One of the great advantages of having additional time is that it will allow you to build your own learning plan suitable for your child. If your child is a 'fast and furious sprinter' of a learner, then tailor the learning plan to take this into account. If your child is a 'slow and steady jogger' of a learner, then try and work a learning plan to suit their ability. Neither Kamran's nor Alice's learning plan provides a set of rules, but each is a guide that offers some structure to help you negotiate through the 11+ process. Here are some points to consider before devising your plan:

- Is your child sitting the CEM, GL Assessment or other exam style?
- Is your child sitting the multiple choice or standard format exam?
- Do you know which subjects will be tested?
- Have you allowed time for consolidation of work?
- Have you allowed time for sufficient practise of new material?
- Have you allowed time for some extended activities to supplement learning?

Here is a CEM style exam learning plan, followed by a GL style exam learning plan for your child. It covers a 24 month period, but depending upon the time that you have left, you could divide the time into days, weeks or months and you can then spread the books and levels equally for the time that you have available. Bear in mind that your child will need time for practice test papers. As you monitor your child's progress, you can update the learning plan if necessary:

CEM EXAM STYLE:		
Month:		

GL ASSESSMENT/OTHER EXAM STYLE:

Month:				

Apply Bond's Step-by-Step Action Plan

Suggested Templates for 12 Month, six Month and three Month Action Plans:

Find the plan that is closest to the period of time that you have, and use this as an overall template for your child's learning schedule.

12 Month Study Plan (for each subject to be covered)

Months 1–3

The First Quarter:

1 Work through the Bond level books at the pace of the learning plan.

2 Use the Bond 'How To Do 11+' series to support unknown areas of learning.

3 Use extended workbooks such as the 'Up To Speed Practice' or 'Stretch Practice' series to supplement learning when it is needed.

4 Begin the motivational planner (see Appendix).

5 Make notes of problematic areas that need further revision.

Months 4–6

The Second Quarter:

1 Continue to work through the Bond level books and the 'How To Do 11+' series.

2 Strengthen problem areas with spelling lists, reading, Bond puzzle books etc.

3 Use the extended workbooks to supplement learning.

4 Revise the learning plan if needed.

5 Continue with the motivational planner.

The Third Quarter:

Months 7–9

1 Continue with the Bond final level books and the 'How To Do 11⁺' series.

2 Introduce strict exam timings gradually in two minute intervals.

3 Continue with the motivational planner.

The Final Quarter:

Months 10–12

1 Revise work in 'bite-sized' chunks for daily revision or use the Bond '10 Minute Test' series to achieve this.

2 Tighten exam timings to allow additional time for checking work.

3 Begin the Bond 11⁺ Test Papers to prepare for the actual exam and the exam format.

4 Practise exam stress busters (see Appendix).

6 Month Study Plan (for each subject to be covered)

First Third:

Months 1–2

1 Work through the Bond level books at the pace of the learning plan.

2 Use the Bond 'How To Do 11⁺' series to support unknown areas of learning.

3 Begin the motivational planner.

4 Make notes of problematic areas that need further revision.

Second Third:

Months 3–4

1 Continue with the Bond level books and the 'How To Do 11+' series.

2 Introduce strict exam timings gradually in two minute intervals.

3 Continue with the motivational planner.

Final Third:

Months 5–6

1 Continue with the Bond level books highlighting any problem areas to work on.

2 Begin the Bond 11+ Test Papers to prepare for the actual exam and the exam format.

3 Tighten exam timings to allow additional time for checking work.

4 Keep to tight exam times.

5 Continue with the motivational planner.

5 Practise exam stress busting (see Appendix).

3 Month Study Plan (for each subject to be covered)

First Month:

Month 1

1 Work through the relevant Bond level books.

2 Use the Bond 'How To Do 11+' series for unknown areas of learning.

3 Begin the motivational planner.

4 Make notes of problematic areas that need further revision.

Month 2

Second Month:

1 Continue to work through the Bond level books and the Bond 'How To Do 11⁺' series.

2 Work at strict timings for each paper gradually in two minute intervals.

3 Use extended workbooks to supplement learning in problematic areas.

4 Continue with the motivational planner.

Month 3

Final Month:

1 Use the Bond 11⁺ Test Papers to get used to the exam format.

2 Keep to tight exam timings.

3 Use the motivational planner.

4 Practise exam stress busters (see Appendix).

Suggestions For Other Timescales

More Than 12 Months To Go:

It is never too early to begin preparing for the 11⁺ by building up all round academic skills. Although your focus might be the 11⁺ exam, think of providing a rich, holistic education for your child. This can be through a broad range of informal learning experiences and also through more formalised learning. Bond starter books for ages 5 – 6 can be used in maths, English, verbal reasoning and non-verbal reasoning as a fun way of introducing logic, reasoning and supporting school-based maths and English. Reading with your child and creating an enjoyable habit of reading a wide range of material, is a brilliant way of providing knowledge and extending vocabulary. Playing educational games, working with measurements and shapes and fun word games keep learning fun. Fostering secure maths strategies suitable for the age of your child and extending a child's general knowledge will prepare your child for any school exam and will encourage a rounded educational experience for your child.

Less Than 3 Months To Go:

If you have less than 3 months before the 11⁺ exam, it is important to focus on exam preparation. Look at exam timings, dealing with exam stress and working through test papers. If time allows, work through the 10 – 11⁺ assessment papers for each subject to be studied to provide some practice at the types of question your child will need to answer. Using the Bond 'How To Do 11⁺' range will provide explanations and examples for every question type to help support your child. Even if you only have days left, working through at least a few practice papers a day plus a few test papers will help. An 11⁺ crash course is not ideal, but it is infinitely better to have some basic exam awareness than nothing. We wouldn't go into a GCSE, A level or even a SATs test without a school providing mock exams and practice papers to recognise the format, the style of question and the timing of an exam paper. Do make sure though that your child is as comfortable as possible and not put under pressure.

No 11⁺ system, no range of books or resources and no tutor can ever guarantee that your child will pass any exam that they sit. Providing your child with the ability to reason, to understand information, to express their self with wide-ranging vocabulary, to read widely and spell competently, to confidently use mathematical strategies and to take pleasure in learning is the best gift that you can offer your child. Supporting their schoolwork and fostering a pleasure at as many learning experiences as is possible is the ideal.

A Guide to the Recommended Material

The Bond range aims to consolidate, revise and prepare for the 11⁺ exams and other entrance exams and for over 50 years, Bond has been the number one series for building towards the 11⁺. Bond has built a reputation on providing consistent, reliable, thorough knowledge through an affordable range of gimmick-free resources. Here are the main ranges that you may find useful:

Bond Assessment Papers

These are the core Bond 11⁺ series books. There are levels from 5–6 years old to 12–13⁺ covering the four 11⁺ subjects with book 1 and book 2 in some age ranges. The Bond Placement Tests will determine what level your child will begin working at in each subject. Each book consists of timed papers that provide extensive practice and constant revision of key areas. Each paper is carefully graded and there is a graph at the back of every book to chart progress.

Bond CEM Assessment Papers

These are an addition to the Bond 11⁺ series to take into account CEM style 11⁺ exams. The books are in English/Verbal Reasoning and in Maths/Non-Verbal Reasoning and span the most popular age ranges. The Bond Placement Tests will determine what level your child will begin working at. Each book consists of timed papers that provide extensive practice and constant revision of the key areas. Each paper is carefully graded and there is a graph at the back of every book to chart progress.

Bond 'How To Do' Series

These books offer specific guidance on how to answer the full range of 11⁺ question types. There is one book for each subject plus CEM English and Verbal Reasoning and Maths and Non-verbal Reasoning books and children can follow the step-by-step guides on how to approach each topic or question type. Examples of each element are provided and short practice activities can be completed to confirm understanding. These books are written for parents to help their child.

Bond 11⁺ Test Papers

These test papers cover all four subjects in both standard format and multiple-choice format in addition to the CEM style test papers. They provide an excellent means of gaining test experience. The easy-to-understand marking scheme offers the best way of gauging how your child has performed.

Bond 10 Minute Tests

The 10 Minute Tests provide bite-sized tests for quick practice and revision of all the key topics and question types for each of the four 11⁺ subjects. Tests focus on individual tricky question types, as well as covering a range of questions in the mixed tests. Each title also includes motivational devices such as puzzle pages and a scoring grid.

Bond Up To Speed Practice

The Up To Speed Practice range provides practice papers for children who find their age range papers a challenge. The questions are carefully pitched to reinforce skills and to provide additional practise for pupils. Each book has focus tests at the beginning of the book followed by mixed papers and a motivational progress scoring grid.

Bond Stretch Practice

The Stretch Practice range provides a more challenging range of practice papers for children who find their age range papers less challenging. They are ideal for the most able pupils or to provide a gentle introduction to the level above. Each book has focus tests at the beginning of the book followed by mixed papers and a motivational progress scoring grid.

Bond Puzzle Books

The Bond Puzzle range provides games designed to reinforce the core logic skills in both verbal reasoning and in non-verbal reasoning. Each book covers the 9–12 age range and can be used by children as an addition to their learning plan as an enjoyable way of learning without realising that they are 'studying'.

Bond 'No Nonsense' Maths and English

These books have been designed in line with the National Curriculum and offer a structured, rigorous step-by-step learning programme for 5–11 year olds. They give essential support for general practice as well as for 11⁺ preparation in these subjects. Maths and English underpin verbal and non-verbal reasoning, so these books can also be used to provide firm foundations for the skills and knowledge needed for these 11⁺ elements.

Bond Online

✓ HINT

Bond is at the forefront of 11⁺ resources, so it is always worth checking any new resources and extensions to their range. Further information can be found on the Bond website (www. bond11plus.co.uk).

The Bond online subscription is suitable for children aged 9 and above and allows children to access 11⁺ Maths, English, Verbal Reasoning, Non-verbal Reasoning and CEM style questions online from any device, anywhere and at any time. They offer unlimited practice, auto-marked tests, instant questions feedback and explanation, progress reports and timed mock tests. Each Bond online test is randomly selected from a bank of thousands of 11⁺ questions to provide breadth and variety.

Budgeting

Many parents will invest a serious sum of money to have their child tutored and prepared for the 11⁺ exam. With the pressure of getting into some grammar schools, you may have read horror stories of super tutors earning in excess of £1000 per hour and with so many tutoring books and systems, can you afford for your child to go through the system?

Tutors, teachers and parents are sometimes cagey when it comes to talking about money and if you browse any bookshop there is a huge range of 11⁺ books offering all sorts of information and practice. Some of these books are fantastic and worth every penny, while others are not at all suitable for a variety of reasons. I used the Bond system for many years before I wrote for Bond and for me, having a simple to use, affordable, comprehensive system that gets top results every time is vital. Looking at any system of books and resources you need to consider the following points:

1) Does the system have a clear, gradual progression through the books from easy to challenging?

2) Is the final book of the series challenging enough for the exam that your child is sitting?

3) Does the system have access to worked examples and explanations to allow you to work with your child teaching them real skills, information and techniques?

4) Is the system tailored to the exam type and question type for your child?

5) Is there the option for extra practice at every level?

6) Are there test papers in addition to workbooks?

7) Are the books easy to use for children, with an easy to use answer sheet for parents?

8) Are all the books in the range easy to buy, affordable and in print?

9) Is the quality of the books and the material in it suitable for a child to work with?

10) Is there an academic heritage that you can trust and feel confident with?

11) Is it easy to build a learning plan that is thorough, logical, affordable and of a suitable quality to help your child receive the results that they are after?

Using the Bond system, here is a genuine learning plan that I devised for Jake to fit in with his family's limited budget.

GL ASSESSMENT EXAM STYLE:	GL Verbal Reasoning : Multiple Choice Format	
Month:	Verbal Reasoning	RRP*
	Bond 'How To Do 11+ Verbal Reasoning'	£9.99
September	Bond VR 9–10 Book 1	£7.99
October	Bond VR 9–10 Book 1	
November	Bond VR 10+–11+ Book 1	£7.99
December	Bond VR 10+–11+ Book 1	
January	Bond VR 10–11+ Book 2	£7.99
February	Bond VR 10–11+ Book 2	
March	Bond VR 11+–12+ Book 1	£7.99
April	Bond VR 11+–12+ Book 1	
May	Bond VR 11+–12+ Book 2	£7.99
June	Bond VR 11+–12+ Book 2	
July	Bond VR Multiple Choice Test Papers Set 1	£9.99
August	Bond VR Multiple Choice Test Papers Set 2	£9.99
	TOTAL COST	£69.92

This Recommended Retail Price was accurate at the time of writing.

As Jake is the eldest of five children, each of his siblings would cost less as the 'How To Do 11+ Verbal Reasoning' would only need to be purchased once. Jake's parents decided to add a three month online subscription to Bond for £17.97 and they have the opportunity to purchase additional books in the Bond range should they wish to. I hope this shows the affordability of using the Bond system and will help provide a guide to help you budget.

> **✔ HINT**
>
> *At the time of writing, a local bookshop had a promotion so the actual cost of the books was £43.28. For £45 Jake had 12 months of books, test papers, a 'How To' guide, one book of lined paper for corrections and vocabulary and a red pen for marking questions.*

Common Questions

Q **What if my child completes a book earlier than the plan?**

They can move onto the next book earlier or you can add something fun to the learning package. (see 'Motivate Your Child' for further information).

Q **What if my child is working slower than the learning plan suggests?**

If your child is taking longer because the work is too advanced, they may need to drop down a level first to ensure there is a strong foundation to build upon. If it is because your child doesn't have the time to complete the homework, look at whether there is an obvious reason (too many hobbies, a period of illness, a hitch at home such as a move or change in the family) and whether things are likely to settle down. If this is not something obvious, does your child feel overloaded with school homework? In this instance, a weekly timetable of priorities is often helpful as well as making sure that your child is not struggling with inappropriate work levels. It might mean that the study plan needs to be adjusted so that your child isn't demotivated.

Q **Do we have to follow the papers in order?**

Yes. The Bond system has been devised so that the progress chart in the back of the book allows everyone to see how your child is progressing. If your child completes the papers out of order or does part of one paper one day with part of another paper then this valuable system is lost. Likewise, filling in the chart after every paper is important to keep motivation and is also an honest and reliable system for showing a child's performance.

Q **What if my child has a really low score in one paper?**

As long as your child scores 85% or more over the whole book, then they are ready to progress to the next level. If they score less than 85%, then it would be prudent to work on the book 2, when appropriate, to give further consolidation at the same level. This also means that if a child is scoring 85% or more, they don't need to complete the book 2 at the same level, unless they would prefer to do so. Please don't underestimate just how vital it is to mark your child's work and to go through their mistakes. If you feel unsure of why a question is incorrect, either use the *How To Do 11+* range of books to help your child or try the Bond Online website for help. When a child understands what the correct answer is, they can learn a valuable lesson from that, which is why consolidation at the end of every book is really important.

How do I build vocabulary?

My pupils have a book and they add to it every word that they have come across that is unknown to them. I then put the definition next to each word and a sentence using the word in context. Pupils can then look through their book and each week or two, I can pick out a word for them to spell, know the definition of, know a word similar to or opposite of and I put a tiny tick over the word that I have chosen to make sure they are all rotated. Of course reading a wide range of material is also crucial to building a rich vocabulary as does playing word games.

My child is scoring less than 85%, should we just move on?

No! If a child is regularly scoring 85% and above they are working at their optimum level but if a child starts to fall below the 85% score line, it suggests that there are learning problems. This is what we are looking for to be best able to support your child. Are the low scores all in one or two question types? If so, they need help to understand this question type. Using the Bond 'How To Do 11+' range can help. Using the Bond Online site or finding a tutor or teacher for a one-off lesson might be worth doing to get over a technique issue.

If your child is losing marks across a number of question types and they are the same types each paper, it may be that your child is already working at their full potential and the material is too challenging for their present ability. In this instance, it is worth consolidating the questions and then gaining some extra experience at the same level using the Bond 'Up To Speed Practice' series or the Bond 'Stretch Practice' series. Stepping back an age group and gaining more experience is often the only step required for a child to gain confidence and to then continue onwards and upwards. If the same age level of work is still scoring low though, it might be worth reassessing whether your child is academically capable of the 11+ test. Is there another school option with a less academic exam that would suit your child better?

If your child is making mistakes across all of the question types and they are different question types each paper, it may be more of a focus or motivation issue. Perhaps looking at the time of study, the environment your child is studying in, whether they are hungry/thirsty/overtired. Are they using sabotage because they do not want to go to the school? (Many children of this age form strong friendship bonds and will try many techniques, consciously or subconsciously, to 'get out of' the 11+.)

Q **Why does my child keep making silly mistakes?**

Try and define the mistakes made and why they are made. Is it that they are reading through the questions too quickly? If so, encourage them to underline the key words or numbers. Are they making mistakes in their calculations? If so, spend time ensuring their basic number skills are strong. Are they rushing though the paper too quickly? Encourage them to get the maximum number of questions correct before they attempt to work at speed. Do they miss out questions? Encourage them to check their work once they have finished a paper to ensure each question has been answered. A tick next to each question checked is a good tip. Although frustrating for you, remember that no child is going out of their way to make a 'silly' mistake and they are probably just as frustrated as you, so trying to break down these mistakes into problems that have solutions is always better.

Q **How do I help my child consolidate effectively?**

As you mark the paper, go through the incorrect answers so that your child understands why it is wrong. If it is a vocabulary or spelling issue, copy it down in a vocabulary book and regularly go through the words there. If it is a maths working out problem, copy the sum out again with another half a dozen of the same type for your child to try again. At the end of each book, copy out all of the incorrect questions and let your child try them again. As these were questions that were all incorrect before, any correct answers this time is a huge improvement. Remind your child that to build genuine skills, it is not a case of whizzing through papers, but of looking to strengthen the weakest areas so that their skills become strong.

Motivate Your Child

motivation action plan preparation
experience direction results
key element success

TOP TIP!

A great tip when marking work is to place a 'C' next to an incorrect question due to a concentration issue, a 'K' next to an incorrect question due to a lack of knowledge and a 'W' next to a question with a working out mistake. This can help a child to see what type of mistake they are making and self-knowledge is a step closer to finding a solution.

❝ *"I love doing the 11⁺ because I get weeks off with no homework and I get to earn prizes. My grandma was so pleased with my progress chart, she let me and my cousins have a sleep over. I took loads of hair bobbles and hair clips that I'd won and we had a brilliant time."* ❞

(Sophie aged 10)

❝ *"I love the Bond Motivational Planner because I never have to nag Sophie to do her work. Every week she works hard at her papers and she knows there are short and medium term rewards for her hard work, and long term, she knows that she will be in the best possible position when she comes to take her 11⁺ test.*

I remember the misery of having to fit in extra homework when I took my 11⁺, but for Sophie it's like a game. She can't see the rest of her future with adult eyes, but I will never again underestimate the power of a sparkly hair clip!" ❞

(Sophie's mum)

The following planner works well with all children. It works on a credit/debit concept so that children can build up credits by doing extra work and then spend this credit on time off or cash it in for 'prizes'. It is successful in promoting self-motivation and deals with the difficulty of keeping children focused. There are two blank grids included in Appendix A, which you are free to photocopy for your own personal use, or to use as a template to create your own grid.

Each week your child will be set their target based on their personalised learning plan. Each time your child completes this weekly target, they can colour in one square of the grid. If they do one extra paper, they can colour in two squares as their target has a score of one square plus one 'bonus' square. If a child completes two extra papers, they can colour in three squares as their target has a score of one square plus two 'bonus' squares, etc.

As a motivating factor for taking care and producing their best, children can be rewarded with an extra bonus square each time they reach 100% in a paper and when they complete a book, they are awarded five extra bonus squares.

Some parents may
feel wary of 'bribing'
their child, but it is
far easier and more
pleasant to reward
than punish and
aren't we preparing
children for the adult
world? For those
of us with even the
most rewarding
of jobs, it might
change the element
of pleasure if we
received no wages
or remuneration for
working overtime.
Children of this age
need to understand
that the rewards
are for doing extra
work than what is
expected of them
normally. They also
need to understand
that it is for small,
hard earned rewards
such as time to
watch a favourite
film, having a story
read to them, family
time at the park,
some stickers or
'pocket money toy'.

This system means a child can choose to colour in the grid quicker than planned and can therefore 'cash in' their grid sooner. Once a month it becomes 'dice week' (although rolling one die is infinitely 'cheaper' than two dice!). When your child rolls the dice, whatever number they roll, that becomes the multiplier of papers completed that week. For example, if they roll a three and they complete an additional two papers, they colour in six squares; two additional papers × three multiplier. Here is an example of Balthazar's Motivational Planner for last month:

Week 1: Balthazar had a target of one maths and one English paper. He completed this and achieved 100% in his maths paper so he received an extra bonus square. (Two squares.)

Week 2: Balthazar had the target of one maths and one English paper. He didn't reach his target for this week. (0 squares.)

Week 3: Balthazar had a target of two maths and two English papers. He achieved this and scored 100% in one of his English paper so he received an extra bonus square. (Two squares.)

Week 4: Balthazar had a target of one maths and one English paper. It was 'dice week' and Balthazar rolled a '5'. He completed his target plus an additional two maths papers and three English papers. He received one target square plus five additional papers × five. (26 squares.)

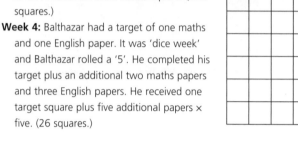

It amazes me how motivating this grid system is. When a child reaches 50 squares they can 'take off' a day of 11+ study and when a child reaches 100 squares they can take a week off and receive a suitable small reward. You will know the type of gift that your child would appreciate most, but the most popular ones at the moment tend to be: arts and crafts materials, time on a games console, stationery, watching a favourite film or programme, trading cards, a trip to the park, hair bobbles, having a playdate, books, having a sleepover, stickers, cake baking and the typical 'pocket money' toys that children enjoy.

Q **Why use a motivational system like this?**

If you are made to work on something every week with no break for month after month, you would soon get fed up and resentful. If you were made to work on something every day and were offered a break and a reward, you would work with a spring in your step and a smile. Children are no different and even when they know it is good for them to spend time on their education, they have school during the day, homework afterwards and then we ask them to do even more homework during the week. It seems better to sacrifice the odd small gift that has been justly earned and to allow them a week of no work.

By reminding your child of their long-term progress, you are making several things clear to your child:

1 You are not disappointed in them

2 The scoring system is a positive way of highlighting problem areas

3 These problem areas can be resolved, which shows effective learning

4 Some papers score poorer than others, which is to be expected

5 The overall score is the important one, not the individual paper scores

5 The aim of education is to learn through our mistakes – this is a good thing

Q **I'm desperate for my child to do well and would feel irritated to see them wasting time on a week off.**

If your child does the bare minimum each week, they will take a long time to reach the 100 squares. If they choose to complete extra work to get there quicker, they are still completing the same amount of work and they need to be rewarded for this. If not, there is no incentive for doing extra. It is important, as a parent, to keep telling a child how well they have done to 'earn' this privilege and to reinforce that it is down to their hard work that they have enough 'credit' to now spend it. You are teaching your child so many transferable skills this way, such as the ability to put in effort now to gain something worthwhile later. You are teaching them to feel proud of their achievements, to emphasise that they are hard-working and conscientious and that they can achieve the goals that have been set.

Q **What if my child is still reluctant to complete work?**

Confirming the need to work steadily in order to achieve knowledge and confidence is important. If your child feels in control of their learning scheme they are far more likely to agree to the regular homework that is needed. Involving them at the planning stage is therefore vital if they are to see what needs to be achieved and in what time frame. Reminding your child throughout this preparation process that they are working well and will soon be able to have some time off, or a prize for their endeavour will keep them focused. Having the grid filled in each week and using the 'dice week' allows them to see how far and how fast they are progressing. It is always worth trying to find out why your child is reluctant. Is their week too busy? Do they want to attend the school? Is the work too challenging? Are they scared of acknowledging the end of their primary school or leaving much loved friends and teachers behind? Are they worried about failing or letting you down? Are you sure that they have the love of education to make the grammar school the best choice for your child?

Q **I know that my child will rush through the papers without consideration in order to achieve the reward. How do I get them to do their best?**

Remind your child that if they achieve below 85% they will have to redo the paper (but still award their bonus mark), but if it is clear that they have rushed the paper and not taken care, they will forfeit the right to their bonus square. Always err on the side of caution here and only do this if you are certain that your child has rushed through the paper. You could always use the '100% gets an extra square' reminder or perhaps add your own variation–for example, if your child achieves 90% of above they will get an additional half a square, or if you have marked their work and the only mistakes are knowledge based, then you will award a square.

Q Can I take squares off when my child misbehaves at home or school?

If a child feels that every misdemeanour will result in reduced squares, the system becomes less motivational and more punishment based. In the same way, if good behaviour is to be rewarding, this is not the place to do it, otherwise the point of rewarding extra 11⁺ work is lost.

Q My child becomes so downhearted when their progress dips below the pass mark. How can I keep them motivated when this happens?

The Bond books have a progress chart in the back, which is filled in each time a paper is marked. Being able to see the long-term view of the progress made, a child can see that the odd paper that achieves less is not a major problem.

Minimise Stress for Everyone

When a child is preparing for the 11+ exam, the whole family are affected. There are ways to minimise potential problems by planning ahead and using the TEAM system:

Time – Expectations – Atmosphere – Management

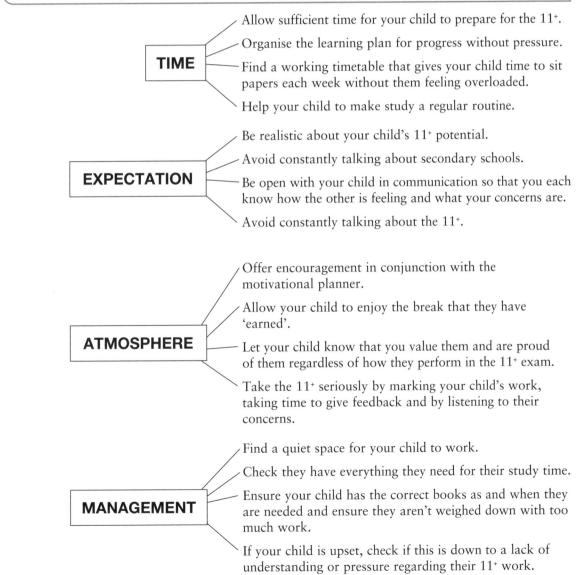

TIME
- Allow sufficient time for your child to prepare for the 11+.
- Organise the learning plan for progress without pressure.
- Find a working timetable that gives your child time to sit papers each week without them feeling overloaded.
- Help your child to make study a regular routine.

EXPECTATION
- Be realistic about your child's 11+ potential.
- Avoid constantly talking about secondary schools.
- Be open with your child in communication so that you each know how the other is feeling and what your concerns are.
- Avoid constantly talking about the 11+.

ATMOSPHERE
- Offer encouragement in conjunction with the motivational planner.
- Allow your child to enjoy the break that they have 'earned'.
- Let your child know that you value them and are proud of them regardless of how they perform in the 11+ exam.
- Take the 11+ seriously by marking your child's work, taking time to give feedback and by listening to their concerns.

MANAGEMENT
- Find a quiet space for your child to work.
- Check they have everything they need for their study time.
- Ensure your child has the correct books as and when they are needed and ensure they aren't weighed down with too much work.
- If your child is upset, check if this is down to a lack of understanding or pressure regarding their 11+ work.

Deal With the Exam Day

There are huge differences between primary schools and how they treat the 11⁺ exam. In some schools pupils are actively coached and given plenty of test papers, while in other schools, your child might be the only one taking the 11⁺ and the school will make no reference to it. Ideally your child will have at least one mock paper under exam conditions and will know what to expect, but if not make sure your child has the following information:

- Your child knows the format of the exam, the subjects to be tested and the date, time and place of the exam.

- Remind your child that they have done practice papers and are used to the format of the exam they are taking.

- Confirm that your child knows how to fill in their name and age on the answer paper although this will be mentioned when they are in the exam room itself.

- Give your child the opportunity to get a good night's sleep.

- Ensure your child gets up in time, has a nutritious breakfast and is feeling as confident as possible.

- Check that your child has a pencil, eraser, ruler, pencil sharpener, tissues and glasses, inhaler or medication if they need them.

- Encourage them to use the toilet facilities before entering the exam room and make sure they know where to go if they need to use the toilet before they start the test.

- Remind them to find the clock before they start so that they can make time checks during the exam.

- Arrive at the exam in plenty of time.

- Wish them well, but remind them that they have prepared sufficiently for this exam, they have worked to the best of their ability and that you are confident that they will now perform the best that they can.

Checklist for Step 3 Success

☐ I've developed a learning plan for my child

☐ I know how to apply the step-by-step action plan

☐ I know how to motivate my child

☐ I know how to recognise and manage stress effectively

☐ I know how to cope with the exam day itself

☐ I still need to find out more about:

....

....

....

....

....

....

....

....

....

....

....

....

....

STEP 4

Manage the Post-Exam Process

- ● Manage the Post-Exam Process
- ● Deal With the 'in-limbo' Stress
- ● Decode the Results
- ● Know What to Do and Say if Your Child Fails

- ● Plan for What Happens Next
- ● Understand the Appeals Process
- ● Prepare for Secondary School
- ● Checklist for Step 4 Success

❮ We had a conditional place – what does this mean and why do we now have to go through the 13+ procedure? Do the exams ever end? ❯

❮ *We had been so geared up in preparing for the 11+ that there was a real anti-climax afterwards. All we could do was sit, wait and imagine.* ❯

❮ I was so glad that we had an effective study timetable in place. This study method really helped my daughter to settle into the homework routine at secondary school. ❯

❮ *Harry passed the 11+ but didn't get into his school of choice. He was devastated. What can we do?* ❯

Manage the Post-Exam Process

Let's deal with the most immediate feelings. You may feel relief that the exam is over and so give your child and yourself time to recover and relax a little. A day out or an activity you can work on together is a nice way of reaffirming the bond you have with your child and can make them feel much less nervous about the waiting period. Reward your child for having worked hard and for studying well rather than just rewarding results. They have just spent months of studying and preparing and an end to this can leave some children relieved, happy and excited, but other children can be tearful, depressed and feeling lost. For many more children, they will go through both sets of emotions as this may well be the first time in their life that they have had such demands made of them and this can be tricky to resolve.

If your child begins to behave in a way that is not their 'normal' self, it is quite likely that they are not their 'normal' self yet and a short time of readjustment is needed before they bounce back. This is rarely anything to be overly concerned with, but if your child does appear to be suffering from extreme feelings or they appear to be struggling to cope, please do take these concerns seriously. What might seem trivial to us may be a major problem for your child. The 11+ exam signals a moving away from the school life that they know, leaving teachers and friends behind, having to cope with a new school with new teachers, new subjects and new friends. They may feel worried if they don't get into a school that their friends are going to or if they feel that they will be judged if they don't get into a certain school.

Symptoms such as prolonged unhappiness, tearfulness, unusual irritability or extreme reactions can signal the difference between the normal patterns of life and the beginnings of an anxiety or depressive problem. Taking advice from your family GP might be the first step to helping your child.

> ❮ *After my 11+ I wasn't worried about the school I was going to, but the school that Ellie, my best friend, was going to. Ellie wasn't sitting the 11+ and she was scared of going to a different school. It made me really sad and in the end I stopped eating and I couldn't sleep. It upset mum a lot. I kept thinking about it all of the time and I planned to run away with Ellie, but I told mum and in the end we sorted it out. Ellie now comes to my house every Tuesday and I go to her house every other weekend. I wish I'd told mum before, but I didn't want to make her sad.* ❯

Deal With the 'in-limbo' Stress

The same feelings of stress can occur during this post-exam period for your child and indeed the whole family. Reliving nightmares or feeling scared of planning for the future is difficult to deal with.

Useful techniques include the **SPLASH DOWN** system:

- Support your child by showing them that the 11+ is only a small part of their life.

- Prepare for secondary school by focusing on new skills or strengthening old ones that will help with the SATs or end of year school exams.

- Listen to their concerns and worries and reassure them that you love them regardless of how they perform in the 11+.

- Achieve skills in other areas of life: encourage your child with hobbies, interests, sports or charitable and voluntary projects.

- Stop referring to your own worries. Your child cannot relax or move on if they are having their attention drawn to your nervousness or concerns. However difficult it might be, try sharing your feelings when your child is not present.

- Help your child to enjoy the remaining time that they have left in their primary school which helps to draw attention away from results.

- Devise plans of what will happen in the event of your child passing the 11+ and if they don't. Focus on the positives of both plans so that your child feels as though they are in a 'win-win' situation and can feel that there are genuine benefits to either option. Encourage your child to take on a role in creating these plans to that they feel empowered and less passive.

- Organise play dates, day trips or activities to enjoy and encourage your child to enjoy the remaining time left in their primary school.

- Write down a reading list after a trip to the library or bookshop. Consider a children's newspaper, such as First News (**http://www. firstnews.co.uk**), a hobby magazine or a comic subscription if your child doesn't enjoy reading fiction.

- Nurture your child physically with plenty of sleep, healthy activity, a balanced diet etc. and nurture them emotionally by looking out for signs of stress, giving space for your child to talk and providing activities or crafts for them to express their feelings etc.

Decode the Results

When do the results come through and what do they say?

The law has changed to ensure that, wherever possible, a child's exam results are available before you have to choose your school. This means that in some authorities the 11⁺ could be sat in the summer term of Year 5 through until the end of October in Year 6. The advantage is that you know the results before you select the school, so there are no wasted school choices on your preference form. The problem is that many parents who might not have risked putting their child in for the 11⁺ now have nothing to lose so the competition can be higher, which pushes up the pass rate. There is also a difficulty with oversubscribed schools as a child may pass the 11⁺ exam, but not get a place in their first school choice. This is one of the reasons why it is so important to make the most of the school preference forms as you can appeal on schools that are entered on the schools preference form, but there is no guarantee that you will be able to appeal for a school if you haven't listed it. With the independent schools the results can take from a week to a few weeks.

When you receive your results it will be a slip of paper with the score, the pass mark and confirmation that you have reached the score to pass. You will then be in a position to apply for the schools of your choice or, if it is an independent school, you can accept their firm or conditional offer.

One of the questions that I am frequently asked is whether to apply for a grammar school if a child has only just scraped a pass. For many parents a pass is a pass, but I think that knowing your child is critical here:

- Has your child only scraped a pass because they have had limited time working at the 11⁺ or have they spent a lot of time studying?

- Has your child relished the pressure of academic exams or has the pressure caused them distress?

- Would your child cope best with potentially being in the bottom of the bottom set of a selective school or potentially being the top of the top set in a non-selective school?

- Would you and your child cope with a range of tutors to ensure they remain in a selective school, especially in those subjects in which they struggle?

- Would your child cope if they were removed from a selective school due to not coping?

- Would your child 'get lost' if they were not being pushed in a selective school environment?

- What school would your child's class teacher recommend?

Although your school is a useful source of information regarding this, your own knowledge of your child is crucial in selecting the best school of your choice. I would also look at the size of the schools, the size of classes, the ethos of potential schools, the reputation of potential schools, the extra-curricular activities of schools, the transport arrangements and the specialism of individual schools. There is an argument in favour of every single school being 'best' at something and 'worst' at something so it is less a case of choosing 'the best school' and more a case of choosing 'the best school *for your child*'.

> ◀ *Elizabeth is a gifted child and had excellent maths skills, had fantastic knowledge of grammar, worked quickly and grasped new ideas with ease. What she couldn't do was non-verbal reasoning. She has poor levels of spacial awareness and just could not cope with the 11+ which was down to a one hour NVR paper. She struggled through the 11+ work and scraped through scoring on the pass mark itself. We knew Elizabeth would do well once she was in grammar school so we grabbed the opportunity with both hands. She is now in year ten and is loving school. She is in the top set for everything. She has taken six GCSEs early and all six were 'A*'s and she is predicted to get 'A*'s or 'A's next year. Thankfully there are no GCSE's in non-verbal reasoning!* ▶

Know What to Do and Say if Your Child Fails

You may have your own way of dealing with any form of failure in your child's life, so this is more for parents who have not had to deal with this situation before. In these instances the following might help:

1) Listen to their feelings and thoughts giving your child the space to feel and think. It can help a child to move through steps of disappointment if their feelings are heard, acknowledged and accepted and they need the space and time to go through this.

2) Explain how football teams fail to win every season, how musicians fail to get a hit record all the time and how top authors fail to get their books printed. People fail in exams and fail to get jobs and failure in relationships and friendships happens all of the time. Failure is a normal part of life and it is okay to fail. This can lead to a useful discussion on how mature they are to be facing this and how they will strengthen a skill that can help them in the rest of their life: to bounce back and to keep trying to do their best.

3) Reassure your child that their result does not, and will never, change the way that you love them and that your only disappointment is for them not because of them.

4) Allow your child to feel as they do, but also encourage them to look towards their future. Hopefully you will have created a plan for passing and failing with positive points for each. If this is the case, then emphasising the positives is the first step.

5) Remind your child that there is no 'best school' but a 'best school for them' and that this is a tiny step on their academic path. Not every intelligent person sits the 11⁺ or passes the 11⁺ and they go on and do extremely well in life.

6) Make plans for secondary school by visiting schools on their open days, find out if any friends are going to your shortlisted schools and make the most of opportunities to broaden friendship circles.

7) Explain to your child that not passing the 11+ does not necessarily mean that they cannot go to the school of their choice. There may be the option for an appeal or for sitting a 12+ or even the 13+ in addition to sixth form applications, so plan for a possible future. In reality most pupils happily settle into their school, but knowing that the door isn't permanently closed can make it easier to accept a second choice school 'for now'.

8) Focus on the strong skills that your child does have. Are they especially good at sport, music, making people laugh, being a kind friend, having leadership qualities, picking up languages, baking, crafts, being responsible, being fun?

Plan for What Happens Next

Once you have your results you are in a position to select which schools you want to enter in your school preference forms. Whether you have received your results before entering your school choices or not, I would stress the importance of applying for as many schools as you can. I have known of parents who chose to write the name of their first choice grammar school for places one to five of their preference form thinking that the LEA will be pleased at how much they wanted their first choice school. I know of others who have only filled in one choice and left the rest of the form blank or have filled in the form, sent back the form and have then changed their mind. Do the research first, take up every place on the preference form with a school that you would be happy enough with if you don't get your other choices and make sure you have sent back the form filled in correctly, by the date given.

If you are applying for independent fee-paying schools, you can usually add this in addition to your LEA school preference form. If you haven't added a school on the form, you cannot appeal for it and the LEA will allocate a school for you. If you are out of area, check the rules first and if the school of your choice is oversubscribed, check the furthest distance away that pupils in the past couple of years came from. If your school states the furthest pupil was 3.4 miles away and you live 7 miles away, your chance of getting that school is remote. You can find this information on your local LEA website and you can also find out how many places the school has available and whether it is an oversubscribed school or not. If it is a faith school it may inform you of how many places are available for children without that faith and the feeder schools.

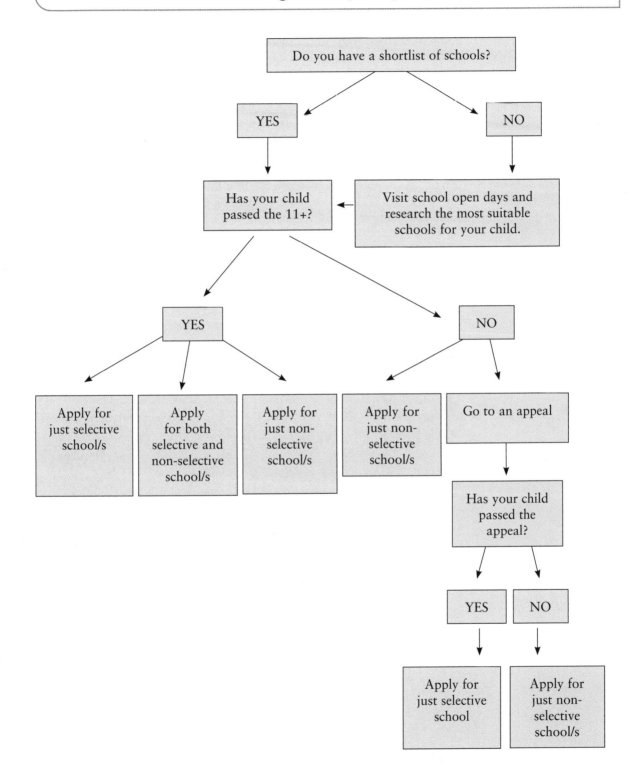

By doing your homework first, you alleviate the problems that many parents come across every single year and will hopefully deal with any potential shocks. You would be amazed how many children are suddenly baptised or begin a musical instrument in Year 4 or 5, how many parents apply to be a governor in the school of their choice and how many parents will rent an address in another LEA to access better schools. Numerous parents will put their home address as next door to the school and even more parents will 'divorce' before applying for a full fees scholarship as a 'single parent with single income'. LEAs and schools are well aware of these 'scams' and many more like this and although some parents will be successful, the majority will not be and the cost and stress of having to prove endless paperwork in an appeals bid, still results in an unsuccessful application. Although it is easy to criticise parents who will go to these lengths, every parent wants to do the best for their child. In some parts of the country, it is the pressure for places in a good school that is driving some parents to try whatever they can to gain the advantage.

> ◖ *We planned our only child's birth for September to give her the best academic chance. We were driven to give her the opportunities that we had had to strive so hard for. We moved house to an area in the country where it was easier to get into a really good grammar school so that we could fund private tuition to give her the edge. We began formal tutoring twice a week in year one. We treated the whole process as a long term goal so that we could be the best parents that we could be. Our daughter did get into our first choice school and we stepped up the tuition to five times a week so that she achieved a perfect set of results at both GCSE and 'A' level. She went to Cambridge to study medicine, which was everything we had wanted for her and we knew that we had done our job. You cannot imagine how it felt when she admitted that she had no positive memories of her childhood. She summed up her whole childhood as "a qualification factory" and she doesn't have much to do with us. We lost our way and cannot believe that we have ended up doing damage to our precious daughter. We are beyond grief-stricken.* ◗

Understand the Appeals Process

One of the most common questions asked is 'What is the pass mark?' and this is soon followed by 'What can I do if my child fails the 11⁺?' Knowing in advance how the exams are marked and what you can do will help alleviate the worry. When you receive your child's school offer, you will also receive details on the appeals procedure and the strict timetable that you will need to follow in order to accept an offer or to begin an appeal. Some of the most common questions about results and appeals are outlined below.

 What is the pass mark?

The number of school places that are available sets the pass mark. If a school has 200 places then the top 200 test marks get in. This does mean that the pass mark can vary from year to year. There will also be variations in the birth rate for individual years, so if there are a lot of boys in your son's year and you have applied for a boys' school, there will be more boys fighting for available places, while girls in the same academic year might have far fewer pupils going for the available places.

 My child is 11 months younger than her friend so how can the marking be fair?

In most 11⁺ areas, exam papers are marked and scores are standardised by age, this means that there are allowances made for the age of the child so that each child can be fairly assessed.

 What does standardisation mean?

All of the exam papers have a 'raw score', which is quite literally something like 78/85 or 69/80 and means the total number of correct answers compared to the maximum score available. Then the child's age is added to the equation and the raw score turned into a grade. A child who has a score of 74/80 and is 10 years and 3 months might get a final score of 130, while a child who also has 75/80 but who is 10 years and 6 months, might also score 130. Obviously there is no definitive answer here as every exam board has their own way of marking that may, or may not, include standardisation.

What is the computer marking system and how reliable is it?

Multiple-choice answer papers can be fed into a computer and marked as the computer 'looks' for the boxes with pencil marks in to award marks. This is a fast system and is very reliable, as computers don't yet suffer with human error. It does mean however, that your child must mark the boxes on the multiple-choice answer sheet carefully.

 What if my child gets just under the pass mark?

There is often a schools' waiting list for the next highest scoring children. Some pupils may have sat the entrance exam for a number of schools and so may opt out of the one you have chosen.

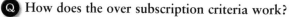 **What if my child has passed the exam, but has not got a place at grammar school?**

This does happen if you have chosen a school that is oversubscribed, especially if your child has scored right on the pass mark. This can be a shock for parents who have assumed that passing the 11⁺ is a guarantee for a school place which is why I would recommend making the most of every possible school choice on your preference forms.

How does the over subscription criteria work?

If a school is oversubscribed, a criterion is put in place to select pupils. You will find information on this in your school prospectus, but the usual reasons that a school will give can include any or all of the following:

- how far you live from the school
- whether your child is in a feeder school
- siblings who may already be in the school
- places for children in care
- places for children with special or educational needs
- children of a certain religious faith
- children with a family connection to the school
- children who have achieved a certain level in music/sports/language or other talent.

Is there anything else that I can do to get my child into the school of my choice?

Some schools have several routes into a school; an academic entrance exam or a music or sport place for example. If your child fails the academic route, is there another route that your child might be eligible for? If not, other children above your child on the waiting list might take up vacant places so that your child moves up a position. Even when the school year starts some pupils will move house or suddenly start another school instead, so if you are really keen to get your child into the school there is an outside chance that a place may be available. However, this can be a stressful situation to be in and you may prefer to end the tension and go for the school offered by your LEA.

My child didn't perform well. What can we do?

This depends on the reason why your child didn't do well. All schools have a policy on their appeals process, and if this is a route you wish to take, you need to contact the school as soon as possible and ask for advice on their appeals system (although when you receive your school offer, you should receive information about appealing and the time frame given). You will probably be advised to wait until the test results are through, but it is wise to inform the test centre as soon as possible after the exam if the reason is illness. If a school is aware that a child took the exam and was then sent to the doctor that day because they developed mumps, it is better than a retrospective appeal three months later.

How can I look at my child's marked 11⁺ paper to ensure it has been fairly marked?

With most examinations (SATs, 11⁺, GCSE, A level etc.) it is not possible for you to see a marked script. There are many reasons for this, including administrative limitations and the psychological effect for a child knowing there may be 'come back' from the parent, however well meaning. The Freedom of Information Act (FoIA) has to be followed by all schools and authorities and they will have strict guidelines on what can and can't be revealed. What you can do is request your child's paper to be remarked by hand, but it is rare for any child to have their score changed because of this, probably because of the accuracy of the computerised marking system.

We waited nervously from December until the results were through on 1 March and we were so pleased that Marie-Anne was offered our first choice of the grammar school. The previous year our eldest daughter Rachael wasn't offered a place because she was short of 3 marks. We had to wait for another six weeks and we had begun to wish we had taken the school offered by the LEA as we were nervous about appealing in case it had a negative effect on Rachael. Then we were offered a place at the grammar school, as we were high on the waiting list. We are so glad we appealed and now both girls are together at the grammar school doing well...

We decided to lodge an appeal because we didn't want Raj to go to any other school and, because he failed to get a high enough mark, we had no other viable option. The whole situation dragged on for weeks and in the end, we were turned down. We tried then to appeal for our second choice of school but that was also oversubscribed and our appeal failed. We really wished we had put more schools down as we were then stuck with the school the LEA wanted us to go to. We still weren't happy and Raj had no school to go to in September. Eventually he went to another school that we were happy enough with, but not until November, and by then he had missed lots of schooling and our childcare arrangements for looking after Raj drove us close to the edge. We found out that you can only appeal against schools you have down on your original list, so when his little brother is ready, we will put down the maximum number of schools and unless he is close to the pass mark, we won't go through an appeal.

So is it worth appealing or not? It is such a difficult decision to make, but I would suggest you look long and hard at the prospectus first. Look at the oversubscription criterion and see how likely you are to be selected on these grounds. Also look at the grade your child has, and if they are very close to the pass mark, it may well be worth appealing. If your child has a low mark and you don't fit into any of the criteria for oversubscription, your chance of appealing is far more limited. It's a difficult balance between realism and hope and there will be many parents who decide the added stress is not worth it. The more parents who make this decision, the more pupils will be removed from the list of potential appealers so bear this in mind if you are appealing.

Prepare for Secondary School

Whatever school your child attends, you want them to be as prepared as possible and that means getting through SATs with as good a grade as possible. In some secondary schools, they will place pupils immediately into academic sets based on the SATs results so it is worth continuing with maths and English to ensure this is as good as possible. Many schools will use CAT tests to enable them to set pupils and the best preparation for this is verbal reasoning, non-verbal reasoning, strong number skills and as wide a range of vocabulary as possible. Reading and using the Bond range of books can help strengthen these skills.

Your child has probably got a good studying routine in place, so this can be utilised with SATs preparation books or the Bond Get Ready for Secondary School series in maths and English. Bond have the 11–12+ and the 12–13+ assessment papers in English and maths and this can help provide a formal structure that your child is already familiar with. There are also a variety of informal ways in which you can help your child prepare for secondary school. Here are some examples that have worked well with many pupils:

LITERACY

- Now might be a good time to get a reading plan in place. This could include a trip to the library or a bookshop and making a reading list that your child would like to work through. Including your child in this choosing process, and in setting a suitable time for their reading, means they are far more likely to take part than in an enforced scheme of work.

- Letter writing can help with extended writing. Encourage your child to write letters to friends, penfriends, children they have met on holiday and family who will appreciate it.

- Keeping a holiday diary, writing journal or scrapbook is another way to encourage extended writing. An appealing book to write in or a writing format downloaded from the Internet can add to the appeal.

- If your child enjoys writing, encourage them to enter writing competitions. The Booktrust website keeps a list of writing competitions specifically aimed at children: **http://www.booktrust.org. uk/books/adults/short-stories/prizes/**

- Playing board games such as Scrabble®, Scattergories®, Articulate®, Who's in the Bag® are all good 'literacy' based games.

NUMERACY

- App games such as Squeebles and Ghost Blasters are great for strengthening times tables.

- The board game Hoo Ha! is another good game for times tables.

- The MathSphere website and the Institute of Mathematics website are great for a range of numeracy games: **http://www.mathsphere.co.uk/ resources/MathSphereFreeResourcesBoardgames.htm** and **http://www. ima.org.uk/i_love_maths/games_and_puzzles.cfm.html**

CROSS CURRICULAR

- Although children will have trips out with school, insurance concerns mean that children are more limited to where and when they go. At this age most museums, especially the 'hands on' ones, are perfect for children and the interactive elements make learning fun.

- Instead of using the computer as purely a games machine, encourage your child to research topics on the Internet. The BBC website is geared up for SATs with educational games and web pages linked to their favourite hobbies or television programmes. There are some fantastic 'brain training' and educational programs online that children enjoy.

- Board games Monopoly®, Cluedo® and Risk® build logic while Trivial Pursuit™ build general knowledge.

- Make the most of any learning experience through practical situations. Decorating a room requires measurement, size and cost calculations as does preparing sufficient food for a party to a given budget. Planning the family holiday (real or dreamed!) is another clever means of developing your child's skills.

- Here are some favourite website that help with interactive learning:

  www.beam.co.uk

  http://www.bbc.co.uk/learning/

  http://resources.woodlands-junior.kent.sch.uk/literacy/index.htm

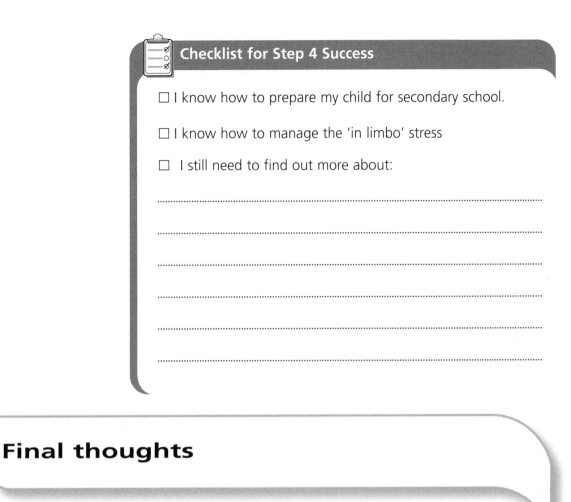

Checklist for Step 4 Success

☐ I know how to prepare my child for secondary school.

☐ I know how to manage the 'in limbo' stress

☐ I still need to find out more about:

....

....

....

....

....

....

Final thoughts

Following the system prescribed in this manual will prepare you and your child as well as possible for the 11⁺ and beyond. The 11⁺ isn't about being a success or being a failure, it's about finding the right school and the right educational environment for your child. Your child might pass or fail the criteria for an individual school's entrance policy, but that doesn't make reference to the rest of their life. There are plenty of bright children who do fantastically well having failed the 11⁺ exam and plenty of children who have passed the 11⁺ exam and are sadly not living a happy and successful life.

Making your child aware that success comes from working to the best of their own potential and reaching their own standards and goals is perhaps the best message you can convey to them. I hope that you have found this book informative and useful and I wish you and your child every success for the future.

Michellejoy

APPENDIX A
The Bond Motivational Planner

These grids can be photocopied for your own personal use:

DATE:											
											10
											20
											30
											40
											50
											60
											70
											80
											90
											100

APPENDIX B
Essential Resources

Summaries of the essential resources that you can use to support your child's 11+ preparations are given here.

The Bond Series:

The Bond 11+ range consists of *How To Do* books, one in each of the 11+ subjects plus two books that cover the CEM style 11+ exam. There are also *Focus On* books in Comprehension and Writing. There are practical workbooks, the *Assessment Papers*, the *Up To Speed Practice* series, the *Stretch Practice* series and the *10 Minute Tests* series. Bond completes the series with 11+ *Test Papers* in each subject, both in standard format and multiple-choice and for the CEM style exams. All of these books can be bought or ordered from bookshops or direct from the Bond website (www.bond11plus.co.uk). Here is the complete list of Bond resources:

Bond Title	ISBN
Bond English Assessment Papers 5–6 Years	9780192739995
Bond Maths Assessment Papers 5–6 Years	9780192740106
Bond Verbal Reasoning Assessment Papers 5–6 Years	9780192742216
Bond Non-verbal Reasoning Assessment Papers 5–6 Years	9780192742209
Bond Fnglish No Nonsense 5–6 Years	9780192740397
Bond Maths No Nonsense 5–6 Years	9780192740458
Bond English Assessment Paper 6–7 Years	9780192740007
Bond Maths Assessment Papers 6–7 Years	9780192740113
Bond Verbal Reasoning Assessment Papers 6–7 Years	9780192740304
Bond Non-verbal Reasoning Assessment Papers 6–7 Years	9780192740212
Bond English No Nonsense 6–7 Years	9780192740403
Bond Maths No Nonsense 6–7 Years	9780192740465
Bond English Assessment Paper 7–8 Years	9780192740014
Bond Maths Assessment Papers 7–8 Years	9780192740120
Bond Verbal Reasoning Assessment Papers 7–8 Years	9780192740311
Bond Non-verbal Reasoning Assessment Papers 7–8 Years	9780192740229
Bond English No Nonsense 7–8 Years	9780192740410
Bond Maths No Nonsense 7–8 Years	9780192740472
Bond English 10 Minute Tests 7–8 Years	9780192740519
Bond Maths 10 Minute Tests 7–8 Years	9780192740564
Bond Verbal Reasoning 10 Minute Tests 7–8 Years	9780192740663
Bond Non-verbal Reasoning 10 Minute Tests 7–8 Years	9780192740618
Bond English Assessment Papers 8–9 Years	9780192740021
Bond Maths Assessment Papers 8–9 Years	9780192740137
Bond Verbal Reasoning Assessment Papers 8–9 Years	9780192740328
Bond Non-verbal Reasoning Assessment Papers 8–9 Years	9780192740236
Bond English No Nonsense 8–9 Years	9780192740427
Bond Maths No Nonsense 8–9 Years	9780192740489
Bond English 10 Minute Tests 8–9 Years	9780192740526
Bond Maths 10 Minute Tests 8–9 Years	9780192740571
Bond Verbal Reasoning 10 Minute Tests 8–9 Years	9780192740670
Bond Non-verbal Reasoning 10 Minute Tests 8–9 Years	9780192740625
Bond English Stretch Practice 8–9 Years	9780192742063
Bond Maths Stretch Practice 8–9 Years	9780192742094
Bond Verbal Reasoning Stretch Practice 8–9 Years	9780192742155
Bond Non-verbal Reasoning Stretch Practice 8–9 Years	9780192742124
Bond English Up To Speed Practice 8–9 Years	9780192740915
Bond Maths Up To Speed Practice 8–9 Years	9780192740946
Bond Verbal Reasoning Up To Speed Practice 8–9 Years	9780192741004
Bond Non-verbal Reasoning Up To Speed Practice 8–9 Years	9780192740977
Bond CEM English and Verbal Reasoning Assessment Papers 8–9 Years	9780192742827
Bond CEM Maths and Non-verbal Reasoning Assessment Papers 8–9 Years	9780192742858
Bond English Assessment Papers 9–10 Years Book 1	9780192740038
Bond English Assessment Papers 9–10 Years Book 2	9780192740045
Bond Maths Assessment Papers 9–10 Years Book 1	9780192740144
Bond Maths Assessment Papers 9–10 Years Book 2	9780192740151
Bond Verbal Reasoning Assessment Papers 9–10 Years Book 1	9780192740335
Bond Verbal Reasoning Assessment Papers 9–10 Years Book 2	9780192740342

Bond Title	ISBN
Bond Non-verbal Reasoning Assessment Papers 9–10 Years Book 1	9780192740243
Bond Non-verbal Reasoning Assessment Papers 9–10 Years Book 2	9780192740250
Bond English No Nonsense 9–10 Years	9780192740434
Bond Maths No Nonsense 9–10 Years	9780192740496
Bond English 10 Minute Tests 9–10 Years	9780192740533
Bond Maths 10 Minute Tests 9–10 Years	9780192740588
Bond Verbal Reasoning 10 Minute Tests 9–10 Years	9780192740687
Bond Non-verbal Reasoning 10 Minute Tests 9–10 Years	9780192740632
Bond English Stretch Practice 9–10 Years	9780192742070
Bond Maths Stretch Practice 9–10 Years	9780192742100
Bond Verbal Reasoning Stretch Practice 9–10 Years	9780192742162
Bond Non-verbal Reasoning Stretch Practice 9–10 Years	9780192742131
Bond English Up To Speed 9–10 Years	9780192740922
Bond Maths Up To Speed 9–10 Years	9780192740953
Bond Verbal Reasoning Up To Speed 9–10 Years	9780192741424
Bond Non-verbal Reasoning Up To Speed 9–10 Years	9780192740984
Bond Comprehension Papers 9–10 Years	9780192742339
Bond CEM English and Verbal Reasoning Assessment Papers 9–10 Years	9780192742834
Bond CEM Maths and Non-verbal Reasoning Assessment Papers 9–10 Years	9780192742865
Bond English Assessment Papers 10–11+ Years Book 1	9780192740052
Bond English Assessment Papers 10–11+ Years Book 2	9780192740069
Bond Maths Assessment Papers 10–11+ Years Book 1	9780192740168
Bond Maths Assessment Papers 10–11+ Years Book 2	9780192740175
Bond Verbal Reasoning Assessment Papers 10–11+ Years Book 1	9780192740359
Bond Verbal Reasoning Assessment Papers 10–11+ Years Book 2	9780192740366
Bond Non-verbal Reasoning Assessment Papers 10–11+ Years Book 1	9780192740267
Bond Non-verbal Reasoning Assessment Papers 10–11+ Years Book 2	9780192740274
Bond English No Nonsense 10–11+ Years	9780192740441
Bond Maths No Nonsense 10–11+ Years	9780192740502
Bond English 10 Minute Tests 10–11+ Years	9780192740540
Bond Maths 10 Minute Tests 10–11+ Years	9780192740595
Bond Verbal Reasoning 10 Minute Tests 10–11+ Years	9780192740694
Bond Non-verbal Reasoning 10 Minute Tests 10–11+ Years	9780192740649
Bond English Stretch Practice 10–11+ Years	9780192742087
Bond Maths Stretch Practice 10–11+ Years	9780192742117
Bond Verbal Reasoning Stretch Practice 10–11+ Years	9780192742179
Bond Non-verbal Reasoning Stretch Practice 10–11+ Years	9780192742148
Bond English Up To Speed Practice 10–11+ Years	9780192740939
Bond Maths Up To Speed Practice 10–11+ Years	9780192740960
Bond Verbal Reasoning Up To Speed Practice 10–11+ Years	9780192742056
Bond Non-verbal Reasoning Up To Speed Practice 10–11+ Years	9780192740991
Bond Comprehension Papers 10–11+ Years	9780192742346
Bond CEM English and Verbal Reasoning Assessment Papers 10–11+ Years	9780192742841
Bond CEM Maths and Non-verbal Reasoning Assessment Papers 10–11+ Years	9780192742872
Bond English Assessment Papers 11–12+ Years Book 1	9780192740076
Bond English Assessment Papers 11–12+ Years Book 2	9780192740083
Bond Maths Assessment Papers 11–12+ Years Book 1	9780192740182
Bond Maths Assessment Papers 11–12+ Years Book 2	9780192740199
Bond Verbal Reasoning Assessment Papers 11–12+ Years Book 1	9780192740373
Bond Verbal Reasoning Assessment Papers 11–12+ Years Book 2	9780192740380
Bond Non-verbal Reasoning Assessment Papers 11–12+ Years Book 1	9780192740281

Bond Title	ISBN
Bond Non-verbal Reasoning Assessment Papers 11–12+ Years Book 2	9780192740298
Bond English 10 Minute Tests 11–12+ Years	9780192740557
Bond Maths 10 Minute Tests 11–12+ Years	9780192740601
Bond Verbal Reasoning 10 Minute Tests 11–12+ Years	9780192740700
Bond Non-verbal Reasoning 10 Minute Tests 11–12+ Years	9780192740656
Bond Comprehension Papers 11–12+ Years	9780192742353
Bond English Assessment Papers 12–13+ Years	9780192740090
Bond Maths Assessment Papers 12–13+ Years	9780192740205
Bond Verbal Reasoning Puzzles 9–12 Years	9780192742230
Bond Non-verbal Reasoning Puzzles 9–12 Years	9780192742223
Bond English 11+ Standard Test Papers Pack 1	9780192740731
Bond English 11+ Standard Test Papers Pack 2	9780192740748
Bond English 11+ Multiple Choice Test Papers Pack 1	9780192740830
Bond English 11+ Multiple Choice Test Papers Pack 2	9780192740847
Bond Maths 11+ Standard Test Papers Pack 1	9780192740755
Bond Maths 11+ Standard Test Papers Pack 2	9780192740762
Bond Maths 11+ Multiple Choice Test Papers Pack 1	9780192740854
Bond Maths 11+ Multiple Choice Test Papers Pack 2	9780192740861
Bond Verbal Reasoning 11+ Standard Test Papers Pack 1	9780192740793
Bond Verbal Reasoning 11+ Standard Test Papers Pack 2	9780192740809
Bond Verbal Reasoning 11+ Multiple Choice Test Papers Pack 1	9780192740892
Bond Verbal Reasoning 11+ Multiple Choice Test Papers Pack 2	9780192740908
Bond Non-verbal Reasoning 11+ Standard Test Papers Pack 1	9780192740779
Bond Non-verbal Reasoning 11+ Standard Test Papers Pack 2	9780192740786
Bond Non-verbal Reasoning 11+ Multiple Choice Test Papers Pack 1	9780192740878
Bond Non-verbal Reasoning 11+ Multiple Choice Test Papers Pack 2	9780192740885
Bond 11+ Standard Test Papers Mixed Pack 1	9780192740717
Bond 11+ Standard Test Papers Mixed Pack 2	9780192740724
Bond 11+ Multiple Choice Test Papers Mixed Pack 1	9780192740816
Bond 11+ Multiple Choice Text Papers Mixed Pack 2	9780192740823
Bond 11+ CEM Test Papers Pack 1	9780192742186
Bond 11+ CEM Test Papers Pack 2	9780192742193
Bond Focus on Comprehension	9780192742315
Bond Focus on Writing	9780192742322
Bond Get Ready For Secondary School English	9780192742247
Bond Get Ready For Secondary School Maths	9780192742254
Bond How To Do 11+ English	9780192742261
Bond How To Do 11+ Maths	9780192742278
Bond How To Do 11+ Verbal Reasoning	9780192742292
Bond How To Do 11+ Non-Verbal Reasoning	9780192742285
Bond How To Do CEM English and Verbal Reasoning	9780192742889
Bond How To Do CEM Maths and Non-verbal Reasoning	9780192742896
Bond Parents' Guide to the 11+	9780192742308
Bond Skills' Spelling and Vocabulary for age 8–9	9780192793775
Bond Skills' Spelling and Vocabulary for age 9–10	9780192793782
Bond Skills' Spelling and Vocabulary for age 10–11+	9780192793812
Bond Skills' Spelling and Vocabulary Stretch for age 10–11+	9780192793843
Oxford Primary Dictionary	9780192732637
Oxford Primary Spelling, Punctuation and Grammar Dictionary	9780192734211
Oxford School Dictionary	9780192756930
Oxford School Spelling, Punctuation and Grammar Dictionary	9780192745378

APPENDIX C
Answers to Bond Placement Tests

To receive a mark, your child needs to have an answer that is 100% correct as there are no half marks given for 'almost' right answers.

Verbal Reasoning Level 1:

Q1	Q2	Q3	Q4	Q5	Q6	Q7	Q8	Q9	Q10
D50	35D	11	32 and 16	6	2	woman	low	mate, team	seat, teas

Verbal Reasoning Level 2:

Q1	Q2	Q3	Q4	Q5
yawned, tired, bed	lights, dark	brief, short	talk, speak	help, less
Q6	**Q7**	**Q8**	**Q9**	**Q10**
in, doors	raw	low	T	H

Verbal Reasoning Level 3:

Q1	Q2	Q3	Q4	Q5	Q6	Q7
shorten	follow	forgive	ice	up	green	down, put
Q8	**Q9**	**Q10**	**Q11**	**Q12**	**Q13**	**Q14**	**Q15**
wilting, hot	turn, wait	green	serve	sheen	3	755	125

Verbal Reasoning Level 4:

Q1	Q2	Q3	Q4
reward, punishment	free, enslave	perfect, flawed	precious, precise, present, prettier, pretty
Q5			**Q6**	**Q7**	**Q8**	**Q9**
graceful, gracious, graph, graphic, graphite			lard	very	soda	MPTF
Q10	**Q11**	**Q12**	**Q13**	**Q14**	**Q15**
IPMF	28	35	tap	Juliet	Juliet and Megan

English Level 1:

Q1	Q2	Q3
I	she	Foul = to break the rules Daffodil = a spring flower Foal = a baby horse Reptile = a cold-blooded animal

Q4

Several = more than a few but not all, Nostril = opening at the end of your nose
Server = one who serves, Smoke = cloud of gas and small bits of solid material

Q5	Q6	Q7	Q8	Q9	Q10
clear	patient	was	drank	helped	did

English Level 2:

Q1	Q2	Q3	Q4	Q5	Q6
drink	creep	Daniel's rabbit	The milkman's overalls	a3, b1, c2	a2, b3, c1

Any two words from the following lists:	Q7
	Adjective: thin, busy, little

Q8

Adverb: stiffly, patiently

Q9	Q10
Noun: birds, branch, father	Verb: sat, waited, feed

English Level 3:

Q1	Q2	Q3	Q4	Q5	Q6	Q7	Q8
b	c	b	c	b	but	so / because	until / so

Q9

Outstanding, outlet, outline, understanding, underline, without, withstanding

Q10	Q11	Q12	Q13
silvery, slippery	library, equipped	might, magazine	tried, separate

Q14 (other examples are possible)	Q15 (other examples are possible)
reminded, reminder, reminding	unequally, inequality, prequalified

---

English Level 4:

Q1	Q2	Q3	Q4	Q5	Q6
To oil or grease	To shorten	To find a solution	castle	tongue	wondered

Q7	Q8	Q9 (Any two of the following words)		Q10
persuaded	father	English, Macbeth, Wednesday, PE		Team, class

Q11	Q12	Q13 (for example)
never / always, best / worst	read / red, seen / scene	step, pace, tread, totter, creep, march

Q14

Tom had asked if he was ready. Tom asked him if he was ready.

Question 15–20 (½ mark each)

The sun beamed down so we packed a picnic of sandwiches, pie, salad, fruit and thick slices of cake then off we drove for a day out. Following the pretty roads, we set off for Llanidloes in Wales. We unpacked the car and settled ourselves beside the lake.

Maths Level 1:

Q1	Q2	Q3	Q4	Q5	Q6	Q7	Q8	Q9	Q10
24	1007	> , >	< , >	40, 79	19, 63	7	49	72	48

Maths Level 2:

Q1	Q2	Q3	Q4	Q5	Q6	Q9	Q10
325	370	2, 3	5, 20	20, 30, 40	15, 30, 60		

Q7	Q8
a) octagon, b) pentagon, c) parallelogram, d) hexagon	5, 15, 45, 55, 120

Maths Level 3:

Q1	Q2	Q3	Q4	Q5	Q6	Q7	Q8	Q9
8.5 10	42 22	36 45	3276	1808	2976	8883	10000	0.1

Q10	Q11	Q12	Q13	Q14	Q15
4.72	A B	E B	48cm^2	143 154	20 30

Maths Level 4:

Q1	Q2	Q3	Q4	Q5
8.01	540	$\frac{2}{3}$	A12, B12, C8	A8, B8, C5
Q6	**Q7**	**Q8**	**Q9**	**Q10**
A6, B6, C5	A54cm^2, B128cm^2	A27cm^3, B60cm^3	£58.85 £11.31	£6.10
Q11	**Q12**	**Q13**	**Q14**	**Q15**
£4.75 £38.75	$3\frac{1}{8}$	$4\frac{1}{20}$	$7\frac{31}{50}$	$9\frac{7}{100}$

Non-verbal Reasoning Level 1:

Q1	Q2	Q3	Q4	Q5	Q6
d	b	d	a		
Q7	**Q8**	**Q9**	**Q10**		
d	c	c	d		

Non-verbal Reasoning Level 2:

Q1	Q2	Q3	Q4	Q5	Q6	Q7	Q8	Q9	Q10
c	c	d	a	d	a	b	c	c	b

Non-verbal Reasoning Level 3:

Q1	Q2	Q3	Q4	Q5	Q6	Q7	Q8	Q9	Q10
a	d	b	c	a	a	d	c	CZ	U3

Non-verbal Reasoning Level 4:

Q1	Q2	Q3	Q4	Q5	Q6	Q7	Q8	Q9	Q10
e	e	d	d	d	b	c	d	a	d